apm KNOWLEDGE

Introduction to

Project Control

Introduction to Project Control

Association for Project Management

Association for Project Management
Ibis House, Regent Park
Summerleys Road, Princes Risborough
Buckinghamshire
HP27 9LE

British Library Cataloguing in Publication Data is available

ISBN 10: 1-903494-36-4
ISBN 13: 978-1-903494-34-9

Cover design by Fountainhead Creative Consultants

Typeset by RefineCatch Ltd, Bungay, Suffolk

Contents

Foreword

In the project management world, project planning and project control go together like the proverbial horse and carriage. So it is not surprising that the APM Planning Specific Interest Group (SIG) has a special interest in project control and hence has produced this introduction to the topic. What is perhaps more remarkable is that APM's publications didn't already include one specifically about control, given that project managers spend such a large proportion of their time controlling projects. So this is a first step in filling the gap.

There is a narrow view of control which is about delivering projects in accordance with their plans, using disciplines like earned value and risk management already championed by APM. That view is about **doing projects right**. This *Introduction to Project Control* offers a wider perspective, which includes **doing the right projects**. It involves integrating **all** the disciplines of project management. Hence it draws heavily on the work of the other APM SIGs, brings together material from the *APM Body of Knowledge, 5th edition* and other APM publications and fills some of the gaps. It should therefore be seen as part of the exciting next wave of APM publications, which started with the guide *Directing Change: A Guide to Governance of Project Management*, in which the various compartments of the profession join forces in a more effective open plan workspace.

This document should be of interest both to those new to the profession and to 'old hands'. It should lead to some healthy debate leading to further publications on this important topic.

Mike Nichols
APM chairman

Acknowledgements

This publication has been prepared by the APM Planning SIG under its chairman Ken Sheard with Neil Curtis as lead author. Contributions have been made by Planning SIG members including Jenn Browne, Andrew Chillingsworth, Martin Eveleigh, Guy Hindley, Allan Jones, Mike Semmons, Simon Springate, Thanos Tsourapas and Paul Waskett.

The Planning SIG is grateful for the feedback it has received from other SIGs (in particular, from Paul Rayner of the APM Programme Management SIG). However, the views expressed are those of the APM Planning SIG and not necessarily those of APM.

Information about the APM Planning SIG can be found at Annex D.

1 Introduction

The *APM Body of Knowledge, 5th edition*[1] defines a project as:

> "A unique, transient endeavour undertaken to achieve a desired outcome."

The *APM Body of Knowledge, 5th edition* defines project management as:

> "The process by which projects are defined, planned, monitored, controlled and delivered so that agreed benefits are realised."

The project management 'process' is a combination of numerous individual processes, many of which relate to the subsidiary discipline of project control. Much of what a project manager does is directly or indirectly related to project control, but the *APM Body of Knowledge, 5th edition* does not explicitly define project control and it is rather difficult to arrive at a concise definition. One possible definition of project control is:

> "The application of processes to measure project performance against the project plan, to enable variances to be identified and corrected, so that project objectives are achieved."

This covers the 'monitored' and 'controlled' elements of project management as defined by the *APM Body of Knowledge, 5th edition* and essentially means "making sure projects are done right". However, there is more to it than that. This publication proposes that an equally important part of control is "doing the right projects", both individually and in programmes and portfolios. This ensures that the projects which are undertaken by an organisation:

- deliver the right products, thereby;
- contributing to the required new capabilities, and hence;
- providing the desired benefits to the organisation.

A wider definition of project control is therefore:

> "The application of project, programme and portfolio management processes within a framework of project management governance to enable an organisation to do the right projects and to do them right."

To achieve this, project control operates across a spectrum from the tactical to the strategic, involving much of the overall discipline of project management

[1] Association for Project Management (2006) *APM Body of Knowledge, 5th edition*, APM Knowledge, ISBN: 978-1-903494-13-4

and involving most of the individual project management disciplines represented by the APM Specific Interest Groups (SIGs).

Since so much of project management is involved in project control, the *APM Body of Knowledge, 5th edition* naturally includes many control-related topics. This publication draws heavily on these topics, developing them and integrating them in an attempt to deliver a comprehensive introduction to the discipline of project control.

Some of the topics are already explored in detail in other APM publications and many of these are therefore referenced. It is not the aim of this publication to reproduce the content of these other publications in any depth, but to say enough to provide an integrated view of control. The definitions used and principles addressed here are broadly consistent with the *APM Body of Knowledge, 5th edition* and with the other APM publications, though some tailoring has been necessary to highlight control principles.

APM's Planning SIG (Annex D) has a particular interest in project control as a natural extension of project planning, which it addresses in the APM publication *Introduction to Project Planning*.[2] The APM Planning SIG believes that effective planning and control are both essential for successful project management. It believes that truly effective control is only possible when effective planning has been undertaken. The ability to control is a consequence of good planning and makes planning an investment rather than just a cost. But the ability to control is also a consequence of the other project management disciplines working properly and so it is probably correct to state that, apart from a few unique elements, project control is a virtual discipline drawing on the others.

Virtual discipline or not, the purpose of this publication is to raise awareness of project control, highlighting its dependence on planning and its relationship with the other project management disciplines. It should be of interest to those new to project management, and hopefully also to the project management community in general and in particular to planning and control practitioners.

This publication addresses five key questions:

1. What is project control?
2. Why control?
3. When to control?
4. Who controls?
5. How to control?

It also defines the characteristics of good project control. It does not include detailed treatment of control tools and techniques, several of which are

[2] Association for Project Management (2008) *Introduction to Project Planning*, APM Knowledge, ISBN: 978-1-903494-28-8

addressed in detail in the other APM publications. The APM Planning SIG anticipates building on its introductions to planning and control by developing in-depth guides, which will contain detailed treatment of tools and techniques used in both planning and control, where not already addressed by APM.

2
What is project control?

2.1 PRINCIPLES

Even the simplest human endeavours require control. Consider, for example, a cycle trip. A cycle trip, however simple, is a unique, transient endeavour; even if you've done similar trips many times before, one of a host of factors may have changed – the weather, the road conditions, the traffic, etc. This time, the weather forecast is for torrential rain, but even so, a loved one needs you to make the trip faster than ever before to bring back some chocolates before a particularly good film starts on TV at 8 o'clock. The core work of this 'project' is pedalling the bike, but a bike is unstable; just riding it requires constant attention to both balance and steering, but you also have to avoid obstacles and navigate. Projects are like cycle trips. They'll take you to your objectives, but only if you stay in control, and it's necessary to stay in control in order to avoid a nasty crash.

Project managers must ensure they control their unique, transient and unstable projects in order to achieve their objectives. Most of what a project manager does during the life of a project has a 'control' element to it: leading the project team, running meetings, managing stakeholders, etc. A lot of these activities rely on leadership skills such as effective communication, influencing, negotiation and conflict resolution (such skills are generally described as 'soft', but they certainly aren't *easy*.) The project manager also needs to employ 'hard', quantitative control processes and it is these that are the main focus of this publication. These processes address all three project dimensions – quality, time and cost, and therefore include all of the following:

- Controlling the scope of the project – controlling change.
- Ensuring that the project's products/deliverables fulfil their requirements – controlling quality.
- Ensuring that activities happen on time – scheduling.
- Ensuring that work is performed within budget – cost control.
- Managing risks.
- Managing problems and identifying issues (and obtaining external help to resolve them).
- Making sure that the project leads to benefits for the organisation.

The control processes involve the collection and analysis of data, the identification of trends and variances, forecasting and the reporting of progress. It is also essential that the information gathered is acted on – without effective responses to actual and potential problems, the project is merely monitored, not controlled. Control is certainly *not* just about control tools or software, although these are generally necessary to carry out some of the control processes. Neither should control be facilitated only by specialist project control personnel: it must be owned and driven by the project manager with involvement of the project team, the project's sponsor, other stakeholders in the organisation and possibly external stakeholders too.

2.2 THE SPECTRUM OF CONTROL

Bicycles are unstable and require continuous real-time control through balance and steering. But making a successful bike trip also requires the bike to be guided around obstacles and to the destination, without getting lost. You control a cycle trip with a combination of reactive and predictive processes. The processes require feedback via balance, sight and sound; some are routine and have become instinctive through experience (like balance); others require conscious attention (like navigation). There is a spectrum of control processes in operation, within which are processes that can be characterised as *inner loop* or *outer loop*.

The inner loop control processes are high-frequency feedback processes operating in real time, and include:

- balance – to stay on the bike;
- vision – to aid balance and to avoid other traffic and obstacles;
- hearing – to sense other traffic;
- kinaesthesia (muscle sense) – to control movement.

The inner loop processes tell you that you're going the right way and pedalling fast enough to be home with the chocolates before the film starts. They also warn of risks (i.e. large lorry overtaking) and problems (i.e. it's started to rain, I've had a puncture and just fallen off).

The outer loop control processes are lower frequency, and may not operate in real time; in the bike trip example, they're mostly associated with decision making and some of them operate before the journey begins, for example:

- choice of destination;
- choice of route;
- choice of transport;
- choice of equipment;
- whether or not to continue.

The inner loop processes are generally applicable to *all* bike trips. They help a particular trip stick to its plan and flag up problems in achieving the plan (e.g. punctures). The outer loop controls are more trip-specific, ensuring that the plan for the trip is optimum, in the light of experience of numerous other bike trips, and if necessary revising the plan in response to trends and events in the journey.

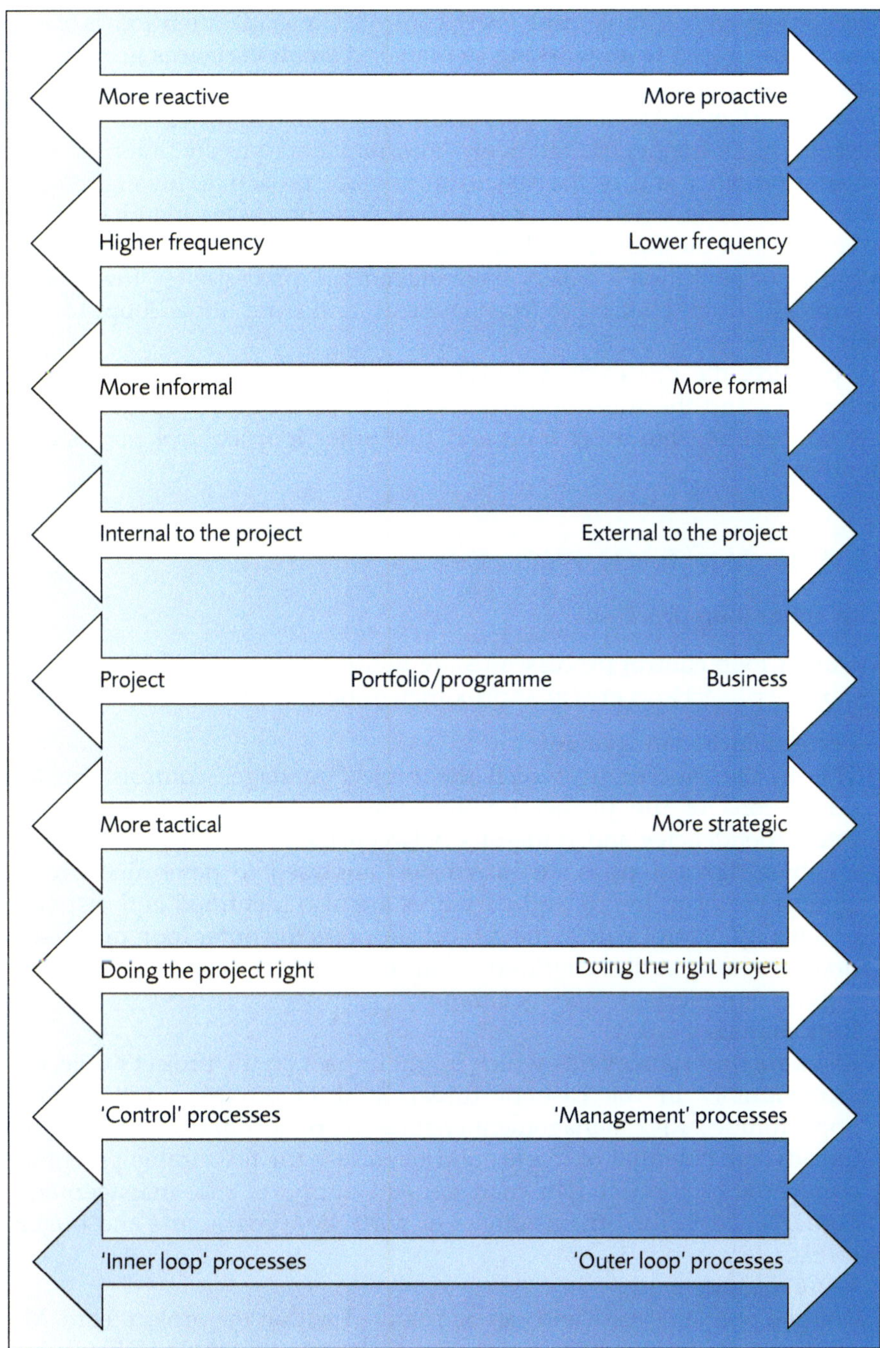

Figure 1: The spectrum of control

Projects too are unstable and need control. Constant attention is needed to keep the project team working to plan and small variances grow to large ones unless the causes are quickly fixed. A spectrum of control applies to projects (Figure 1). At one end of the spectrum the processes are mostly reactive, high frequency, relatively informal and largely internal to the project; the other end of the spectrum is more proactive, lower frequency, more formal and external to the project. The processes blend from pure project control through control/management of portfolios and programmes into the organisation's business management processes – from tactical to strategic, from 'control' to 'management' and from 'inner loop' to 'outer loop'.

In practice, the processes are highly interdependent, making both their boundaries and the transition from inner loop to outer loop indistinct. In this publication, five inner loop and five outer loop control processes are identified.

2.3 THE CONTROL PROCESSES

2.3.1 Inner loop processes

The inner loop control processes reside within the day-to-day implementation of the project and are (in approximate innermost to outermost order):

1. **Performance management**
   This is the process by which the project manager controls the three dimensions of the project (quality, time and cost) and manages the interdependencies and trade-offs between them. Actual performance in all three dimensions is measured and analysed to determine progress against the plan; trends and variances are also identified and responded to. Quality control within the project supports the outer loop processes of quality assurance and continuous improvement. The control of the timing aspects of projects is called *scheduling*.
2. **Risk management**
   Risks are uncertain events which might impact on the project's objectives, unfavourably in the case of threats and favourably in the case of opportunities. Risk management enables the project manager to minimise the adverse potential of threats and maximise the favourable potential of opportunities. Project risk management supports risk management at higher levels in the organisation – at portfolio/programme and business levels.
3. **Issue management**
   Routine problems arise and can be resolved within the project team. More severe problems require external assistance to resolve them. Issue management escalates issues to obtain external support to ensure the

rapid and effective resolution. (Note that while issue management resides within the project as one of the inner loop processes, the assistance obtained comes from outside.)

4. **Review**
   Review brings together the outputs of performance management, risk management and issue management to create an holistic overview of the status of the project. It brings into focus the performance trends and variances and the risks and problems that are significant: this enables the project manager to prioritise responses. The involvement of the project sponsor and other key stakeholders enables them to exercise due diligence and to provide advice and assistance when necessary. It enables the organisation to ensure that it is doing the project right.
5. **Change management**
   Project planning and execution are almost invariably imperfect. Changes to the project are required to ensure that it achieves its objectives; such changes are internal to the project. Also the objectives themselves may be changed by the organisation or the client; these are external changes. Whether internal or external, changes must be managed to ensure that the desired outcomes are achieved, with the least disruption possible.

2.3.2 Outer loop processes

While the inner loop control processes reside within a single project, the outer loop control processes wrap around all the organisation's projects (Figure 2). They provide the organisational framework and context within which individual projects are undertaken.

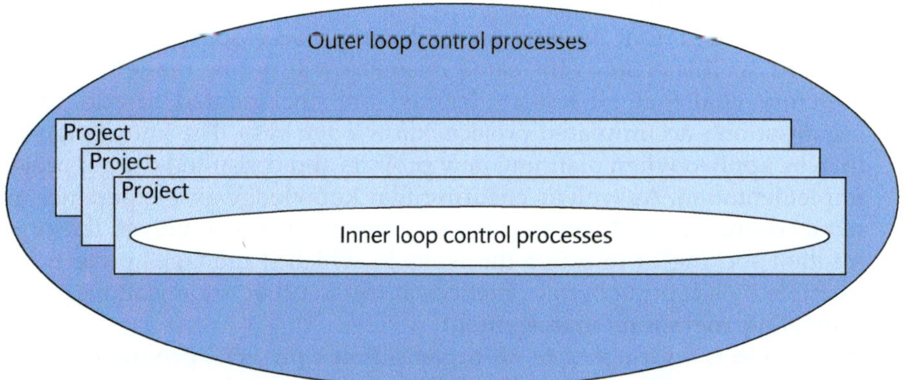

Figure 2: The relationship between inner loop and outer loop control processes

The outer loop control processes, again in approximate innermost to outermost order, are:

1. **Quality assurance**
   Project quality management ensures that both the outputs of a project and the means by which they are realised meet the needs of stakeholders. Quality management involves quality planning, quality control, quality assurance and continuous improvement. Quality planning is the part of project planning which ensures that the project management plan defines a project implementation capable of delivering satisfactory outputs and includes appropriate quality control. Quality control is part of the inner loop performance management process. Quality assurance, identified here as an outer loop control process, provides confidence that the project's quality requirements can be achieved, by validating the consistent use of procedures and standards. This is achieved by independent reviews and formal audits of the project. The remaining quality management process is continuous improvement (see point 3 below).
2. **Life cycle management**
   All projects have a life cycle (Section 4.1). Life cycle management formalises the life cycle and ensures that individual projects follow the life cycle. This is done by critically examining a project at defined points. Such a process ensures a consistency of approach to projects and enables them to be challenged (in formal gate reviews) for planning maturity, bounded risk, sound business cases and implementation performance. Insufficiently planned or unduly risky projects can be returned for additional planning. Projects with poor business cases can be rejected or returned for re-definition. Poorly-performing projects can be re-directed or in extreme cases terminated. This enables the organisation to filter out and avoid further expenditure on projects that are unlikely to produce a worthwhile return.
3. **Continuous improvement**
   It is important that lessons learned on predecessor projects are fed forward, as this ensures the same mistakes will not be made twice. It is therefore vital that all lessons learned are documented to add to the organisation's accumulated projects knowledge base. The knowledge can then be applied when planning new projects and consulted during project implementation. As well as ensuring that knowledge and experience are retained and re-used, continuous improvement also involves the organisation seeking to improve the ways in which it manages projects, for example by adopting better practices in use in other organisations.
4. **Portfolio/programme management**
   A portfolio is a grouping of an organisation's projects, programmes and business-as-usual activities. Portfolio management is the selection and management of a portfolio grouping taking into account resource constraints such as the availability of internal funding for organisational

changes. A programme is a group of related projects which collectively are necessary for the achievement of a strategic change. Programme management is the coordinated management of related projects so that interdependencies are achieved and products of individual projects contribute to the realisation of a new capability for the organisation or its client. Portfolio management and programme management are different but sometimes confused, since both coordinate projects to achieve desirable business outcomes. A key difference is that within a programme, the projects are interdependent and all contribute to the new capability, so that cancellation or failure of one project directly impacts the others and hence impacts on the overall programme objectives; programme management is therefore essential. Within a portfolio, the projects are less interdependent and the consequences of cancellation or failure are more localised; portfolio management, while desirable, is therefore not essential. The disciplines of portfolio management and programme management are linked in this publication only because of some similarities in their roles in project control, particularly with regard to 'doing the right projects'.

5. **Governance of project management**
   Corporate governance provides the structure through which the objectives of an organisation are set, the means of attaining those objectives is determined and performance towards achieving the objectives is monitored. The governance of project management concerns those aspects of corporate governance that are specifically related to project activities. Effective governance of project management ensures that an organisation's project portfolio is aligned with the organisation's objectives, is effectively delivered and is sustainable. It manages business risk, including the collective risk to the business posed by the organisation's portfolio(s). It also ensures that the organisation's board is provided with timely, relevant and reliable information about its projects, programmes and portfolio(s). While governance of project management is a subset of corporate governance, it also includes the governance of project management processes which are outside the direct concern of corporate governance. By ensuring that the project management processes are operating effectively, it ensures that the organisation's projects are effectively controlled and that its portfolios/programmes are effectively directed.

Portfolio management, programme management and the governance of project management are all much more than control processes; their identification here as outer loop control processes is intended only to explain their roles in project control.

Stakeholders outside the project team are heavily involved in all the outer loop processes, which collectively enable the organisation to ensure that it is both doing projects right and doing the right projects. The outer loop processes rely on the outputs of the inner loop processes and simultaneously test that the inner loop processes are working effectively. Figure 3 shows all of the control processes on the spectrum of control. *Risk management at portfolio/programme and business levels are beyond the scope of this publication.*

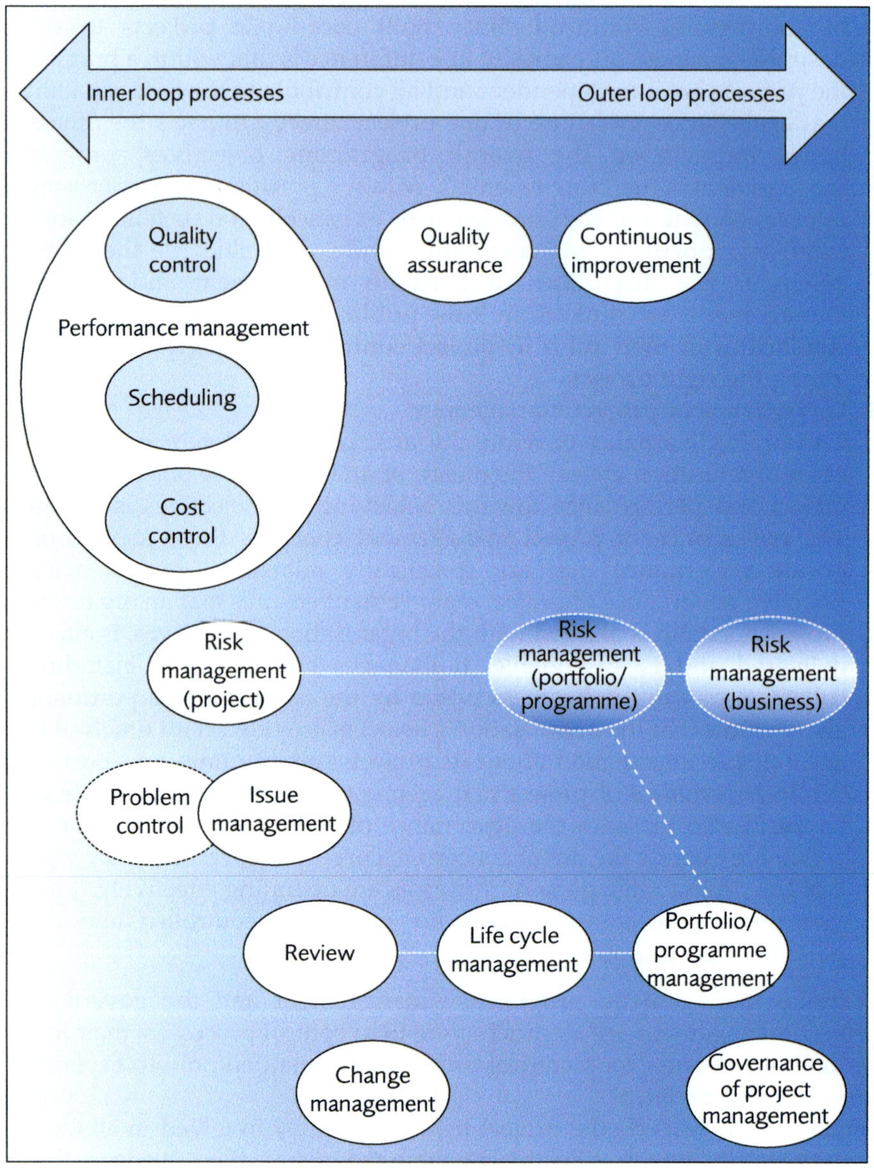

Figure 3: The control processes

2.4 RELATIONSHIP TO BUSINESS PROCESSES

The inner loop control processes wrap around the core work of projects, and operate within the framework for projects provided by the outer loop control processes. Both sets of control processes operate within an infrastructure of other processes needed by the organisation, some project-related and others necessary for non-project activities ('business as usual'). Some of these business processes are identified in Figure 4. They are outside the scope of this publication, except for a few general observations:

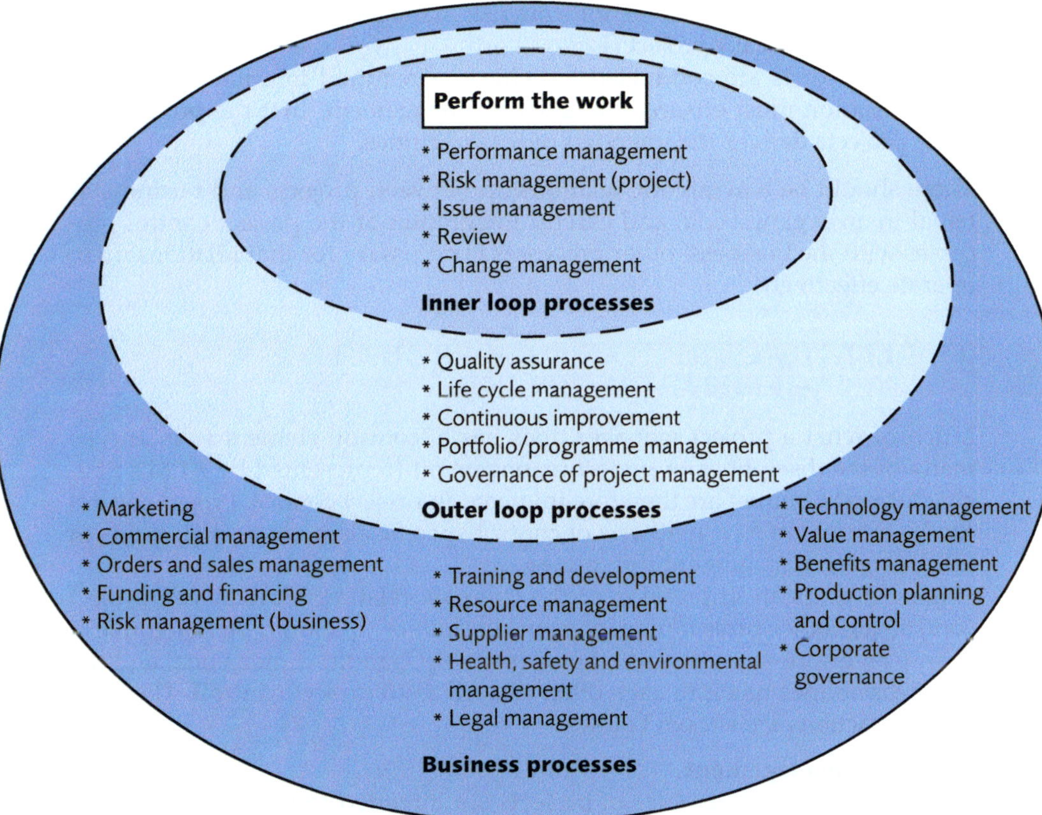

Figure 4: Relationship to business processes

- Project control in particular and project management in general rely on outputs from the other business processes. Thus the intake of client orders via orders and sales management provides project budgets via funding and financing. Training and development ensure that suitably qualified personnel are available in the organisation; resource management ensures that suitably qualified and experienced personnel are assigned to project teams when required and are re-assigned to other projects or to business as usual tasks when projects finish.

- The other business processes rely on outputs from project management in general and from project control in particular. For example the training and development process requires information about medium and long term skills requirements for forthcoming projects, via portfolio/programme management. Scheduling within the performance management process informs the resource management process of imminent changes in resource requirements. Project risk management, via risk management at portfolio/programme level, informs risk management at business level of the most significant project risks.
- Where projects are conducted to achieve a required internal change, the organisation must ensure, via benefits management, that the products of the projects deliver the intended new capabilities.

There should be a symbiotic relationship between projects and business as usual in an organisation, and careful integration of the project control processes with the business' other processes is necessary for that relationship to operate effectively.

2.5 RELATIONSHIP TO OTHER PROJECT MANAGEMENT DISCIPLINES

Much of what a project manager does has a 'control' element to it, and so many of the disciplines of project management (represented by APM's Specific Interest Groups) are therefore involved in project control. Project control can be thought of as a synthesis of control-specific elements and elements of other project management disciplines.

Figure 5 gives an impression of the complex relationship between project control and other project management disciplines (it should be noted that it is only an impression, because the relationship is multi-dimensional and the other disciplines relate to each other as well as to project control). The various interactions are shown below:

- **Benefits management**
  The products/deliverables of projects are intended to be of benefit to the organisations for which the projects are being implemented. The intended benefits should be enshrined as project objectives during project planning; continuing focus on benefits informs control decisions such as trade-offs between quality, cost and time and about whether to modify project objectives via change management.
- **Contracts and procurement**
  Unless a project is undertaken wholly within an organisation, the success of the project depends on the performance of subcontractors. Contracts

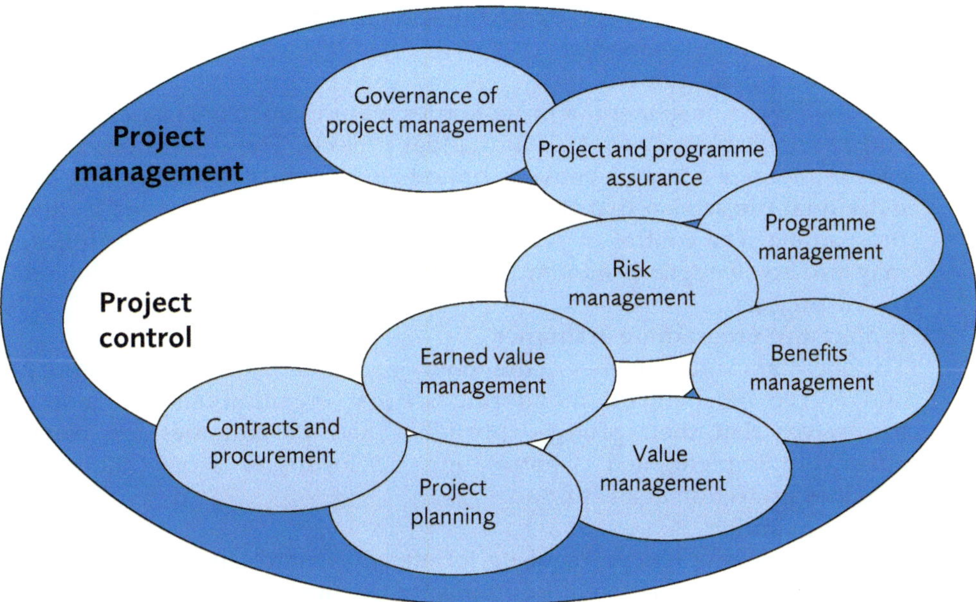

Figure 5: Relationship to other project management disciplines

and procurement ensure that scopes of supply and scopes of work are suitability placed with subcontractors. It also ensures that relationships and procedures are in place to control the performance of subcontractors therefore enabling project objectives to be achieved.

- **Earned Value Management (EVM)**
  EVM is the single most powerful performance management technique that can be employed in project control. It measures the performance of the project against the plan to provide early identification of variances (current and projected), which can then be corrected to keep the project on track.
- **Governance of project management**
  Good governance requires that projects have effective control processes and lays down many of the required attributes of those processes. The operation and outcomes of the review and life cycle management processes in particular demonstrate to the organisation that projects are well-governed. They also show that project management is working efficiently and effectively and satisfying disclosure and reporting requirements.
- **People**
  Above all, effective control depends on people: individually, in teams and in the whole organisations. Effective control cannot be achieved unless the organisational culture in which a project team operates enables it, and nor

can it be achieved without the communication, influencing and other 'soft' skills of the project manager.

- **Programme management**
  The effective management of programmes requires effective management, and hence effective control, of individual projects. The control processes enable interdependencies between projects to be managed, integrating the individual projects so that the required benefits can be delivered by the programme. The control of projects within programmes (and portfolios) may also involve setting standards and mandating processes to be adopted by the projects.
- **Project and programme assurance**
  The operation and outcomes of the control processes provide transparency and enable independent monitoring so that organisations can assure themselves that their projects, portfolios and programmes are being effectively implemented. Control and disclosure of project finances provides protection against fraud.
- **Project planning**
  Effective planning is a prerequisite for effective control, because the plan defines how the project will be implemented (including its control processes) and provides the baseline against which performance is measured. During project implementation, planning is central to the change management process, defining internal and external changes to the project.
- **Risk management**
  Risk management is one of the inner loop project control processes, enabling projects to minimise the adverse potential of threats and to maximise the favourable potential of opportunities. Risk management of individual projects supports portfolio/programme and business risk management.
- **Value management**
  This helps define projects that best meet the needs of an organisation and is concerned with motivating people, developing skills, advancing teams and promoting innovation in order to optimise project performance. It improves the framework for project control decisions.

2.6 THE ROLE OF THE PROJECT MANAGEMENT PLAN

A bike trip should start with some sort of plan, whether simple or complex, e.g. for a quick trip to the shops or for an entry in the Tour de France. Pre-journey planning should have confirmed the need for the trip; determined that the bike, rather than an alternative form of transport, is the best way to get to the destination; estimated how long the trip will take, etc.

Projects need plans, too. A project management plan (PMP), prepared by project planning, defines a project in terms of why, what, how, how much, who, when and where:

- 'Why?' is a statement of the change to be delivered by the project, which includes a definition of the need, problem or opportunity being addressed and the benefits to be delivered.
- 'What?' describes the objectives, a description of the scope, the deliverables and their acceptance criteria. It also describes the success criteria for the project and the key performance indicators that will be used to monitor its progress. The 'what?' needs to take into account the project's constraints, assumptions and dependencies.
- 'How?' defines the strategy for management and execution of the project, its handover, the processes, resources (people, facilities, equipment, tools and techniques) to be used, including the project control arrangements.
- 'How much?' defines the project's cost and budget, the breakdown of the budget and the cost control process.
- 'Who?' includes a description of key project roles and responsibilities and of the resources that will be required during implementation, including those of subcontractors.
- 'When?' defines the project's sequence of activities and timescales, including milestones and phases/stages.
- 'Where?' defines the geographical locations where the work will be performed, which impacts on resources, timescale and cost.

The PMP is progressively developed during planning and is subsequently managed as a live, configuration-controlled document. Once agreed, the PMP provides a baseline description of how the project will be implemented, it is then periodically reviewed and updated through change management. This is especially important where a contractual relationship exists between the project organisation and a client.

A good PMP is vital for effective control because it defines 'the management' and 'the plan':

- The 'management' elements of the PMP, principally addressing 'how', 'who', and 'where', define the implementation of the project.
- The 'plan' elements of the PMP, principally addressing 'what', 'how much' and 'when', define the baseline against which project performance is measured.

Project control measures variances to 'what', 'how much' and 'when' and applies corrections via 'how', 'who' and 'where'.

3
Why control?

3.1 REASONS FOR CONTROL

The fundamental reason for control is to maximise the chances of project success, through achievement of the project's objectives, and to demonstrate that success has been achieved.

There are numerous additional reasons:

a) **To keep the project on track.** Without control, projects can quickly go off track: some or all of the objectives will suffer. The 'track' is defined by the project management plan, in which the organisation should have invested considerable planning time and resources in order to maximise the likelihood of project success. The project should therefore be implemented in accordance with the PMP, until such time as feedback from the control processes demonstrates that changes to the plan are necessary. The plan can then be re-optimised, via change management, establishing a modified track for the remainder of the project.

b) **To anticipate and avoid problems.** Risk management, trend analysis and forecasting are proactive elements of project control which can be used to identify problems before they occur and avoid them, or identify opportunities and realise them. Continuous improvement seeks to avoid revisiting problems experienced on predecessor projects.

c) **To detect and react promptly when problems do arise.** Problems inevitably occur and when they do it is best if they are promptly detected and corrected before they worsen. The PMP defines what should be happening on a project. Without this baseline for the project it may be much harder actually to identify that something is going wrong – until the symptoms have become so severe that they're impossible to miss, and by then very difficult to cure. So, for example, quality control can promptly detect defective products, enabling corrective action to be implemented before the cost of rework becomes excessive. Monitoring of actual costs can identify misbookings and correct them before project budgets are exceeded, or without the need for extensive unnecessary cost transfer effort. Schedule reviews identify if activities begin to slip.

d) **To maintain commitment.** Projects require commitment from everyone concerned. The project planning process should have delivered a PMP which has buy-in from the project team and other stakeholders. Controlling the project to the plan and providing visibility that it is happening ensures commitment is maintained. Project objectives may be defined as personal performance objectives and used to reward success, but the success of reward-for-performance depends on the effective and fair measurement of performance. Review by the sponsor and project board demonstrates that the project remains of interest to the organisation. What gets measured gets done.

e) **To facilitate effective communication.** Communication is important to effective project management and all but the most trivial projects require specific management. The PMP defines the objectives of the project and how it will be implemented. On larger or more complex projects, it should define specifically how project communications will be managed. Elements of the plan communicate particular information, for example the schedule communicates when activities must occur, so that resource availability can be managed.
f) **In response to contractual requirements.** The contract under which the organisation is undertaking a project for a client may include specific requirements for project control, such as the nature and frequency of reviews and the type of information to be presented. The contract may specify the use of EVM, and may even base progress payments on earned value.
g) **In response to compulsory requirements.** Previously, organisations might only have had to produce formal accounts, but compulsory requirements now extend into the project management arena in general and control in particular via, for example, ISO standards and corporate governance requirements. A projects-based organisation must meet relevant standards if it is to continue to operate.
h) **To avoid reputational damage, loss of business and litigation.** Organisations whose business is in projects must succeed in projects in order to avoid adverse publicity, damage to their reputation and probable loss of business. Failed projects may result in liquidated damages and in extreme cases in legal claims against the project organisation.

3.2 REASONS PROJECTS FAIL

There are many reasons why projects fail. Project control directly addresses several of the common ones:

a) **Scope creep.** The scope of a project is defined by its deliverables and by the work necessary to realise those deliverables. The project's objectives summarise the scope, define the quality of the deliverables and define the time and budget within which the project must be completed. Scope creep occurs when the range and/or quality of the deliverables increases without formal recognition of the associated impact on the scope of work and the time and budget objectives. Imprecise or changing user requirements are two of the root causes of scope creep. Rigorous change management, supported by effective management of requirements, ensures that changes are identified and are either rejected or are accepted formally by the key stakeholders, with due recognition of their impact on project objectives.

b) **Inadequate resources.** Projects need resources of many kinds: suitably qualified and experienced personnel, materials, manufacturing and test facilities and, above all, money. Resources are generally scarce – organisations must be lean to survive in competitive business environments – and there is often competition for resources between projects, between portfolios/programmes and with non-project activities. Good project planning ensures that the resources required are fully defined in the PMP and agreed by the key stakeholders. Good project control can then ensure that the required resources are available when needed by the project, manage resource interdependencies between projects and re-plan in response to resource availability problems. Key to this are scheduling (the up-to-date resourced schedule shows when resources are required), risk management (to identify and respond to resource availability threats) and issue management (to obtain assistance when resource problems cannot be resolved within the project).
c) **Late identification of variances.** Variances from plan are almost inevitable. If adverse variances are identified promptly, there is a much greater likelihood of effective response. If they are identified late, they are likely to have grown to a size where no practical response can avoid adverse impact on project objectives. Good performance management (particularly EVM) ensures the early identification of variances. Good risk management may enable potential causes of adverse variances to be avoided.
d) **Issues not managed.** Even with good project management and effective project control, problems do arise that cannot be resolved within the project. Issue management enables such problems to be escalated as issues so that external assistance can be obtained. Without an effective issue management process, or in an organisation whose culture does not provide an appropriate balance of challenge and support, issues may be suppressed until damage to the project's objectives is unavoidable.

Poor governance in general and ineffective sponsorship in particular are often identified as contributing to project failure; both are addressed by ensuring that effective governance of project management is operating.

3.3 RELEVANCE TO DIFFERENT TYPES OF ORGANISATION

Control is important in different ways to different types of organisation. The details are outlined below.

3.3.1 The client organisation

A client organisation requires the products/deliverables of a project for the new capabilities and benefits they will provide and pays for the project. It chooses not to implement the project itself, perhaps because it lacks the necessary competencies in house and therefore selects a contractor organisation to undertake the project on its behalf. Examples of client organisations include:

- a high street bank which requires new account management software;
- a train operating company which requires a new signalling system;
- a ministry of defence which requires a new air defence system for its nation's air force.

The client organisation owns the business case for the project, and, in order to act as an informed customer, must ensure that its contractor is fulfilling its obligations under the project's contract. The contractor may have been selected *inter alia* because of its good track record in project management, based on effective project control. The client organisation must now make sure its project is being controlled effectively. The client organisation's control processes therefore include assuring the contractor's control processes and receiving regular progress reports to demonstrate that the project remains on track to deliver its objectives.

3.3.2 The contractor organisation

A contractor organisation specialises in implementing projects for clients. Having secured contracts, it needs to implement projects successfully to avoid damage to its reputation and to position itself for repeat and related business. The contracts are likely to have been obtained through competitive tendering and in a challenging business environment, financial margins are likely to be tight. Project planning will have generated a plan on which the contractor's bid is based, including a cost estimate and a price build up; the bid price reflects the costs plus a financial margin to cover business costs and provide profit. Controlling the project in accordance with the plan is necessary, both to realise the products the client needs while simultaneously achieving (and ideally, improving on) the financial margin.

3.3.3 The in-house projects organisation

An in-house projects organisation requires the products of the project for the capabilities and benefits they will deliver, and owns the business case. It pays for the project and chooses to implement the project itself, having the necessary competencies and available resources in house to do so. The project management plan defines the project objectives and the resources and processes required to achieve those objectives. The in-house projects organisation uses its own resources, and its own funds, to achieve the desired changes, it needs good project control to ensure that the desired changes are achieved expeditiously and cost-effectively and to ensure that the business case is delivered.

4
When to control?

4.1 THE PROJECT LIFE CYCLE

A project is a transient endeavour with a start and a finish, and between these events it goes through several distinct phases which constitute the project life cycle. The focus of project management in general and of project control in particular changes from phase to phase, so an understanding of the life cycle is vital. Some organisations fail to distinguish the phases or skimp some of them, to the detriment of effective project management. Not all projects make it all the way through the life cycle; some projects should not be implemented at all because their business cases are inadequate and others may have to be terminated because of changing circumstances or poor performance.

Each project is unique but there is much commonality between the life cycles of projects. It is possible to define and apply a generic life cycle to an organisation's projects. Life cycle management ensures adherence to the organisation's life cycle model and brings rigour and discipline to the organisation's projects.

The project life cycle model in the *APM Body of Knowledge, 5th edition* consists of the following phases: concept; definition; implementation; handover and closeout. The *APM Body of Knowledge, 5th edition* regards handover and closeout as a single phase and notes that some projects are extended to include operation and termination phases. *Termination covers the disposal of project products/deliverables at the end of their useful life.* Logically, closeout should be the last phase of the project, whatever phases precede it, so here closeout is shown as a phase in its own right, separate from handover (Figure 6A).

This publication uses a modified life cycle model consisting of concept, definition, mobilisation, implementation and closeout phases, and features a pre-project initiation phase (Figure 6B). The initiation and mobilisation phases are introduced because of their importance to project control, having distinct control needs different from the other phases. Mobilisation *could* be regarded as the first stage of the implementation phase, but insofar as closeout is regarded as a separate phase, it seems appropriate to regard mobilisation as one too. In this alternative life cycle model, product realisation, handover, operation and disposal are considered to be stages of the implementation phase. Disposal deals with decommissioning and removing products from operational use: disposal (stage) is used in place of termination (phase) because here 'termination' is taken to mean stopping a project before its normal finish. After initiation, a project starts at the beginning of the concept phase and normally finishes at the end of the closeout phase, after full implementation. A *terminated* project is stopped early, omitting some of the phases or stages, but nevertheless should be properly closed out. Such a project should contain important lessons for the organisation.

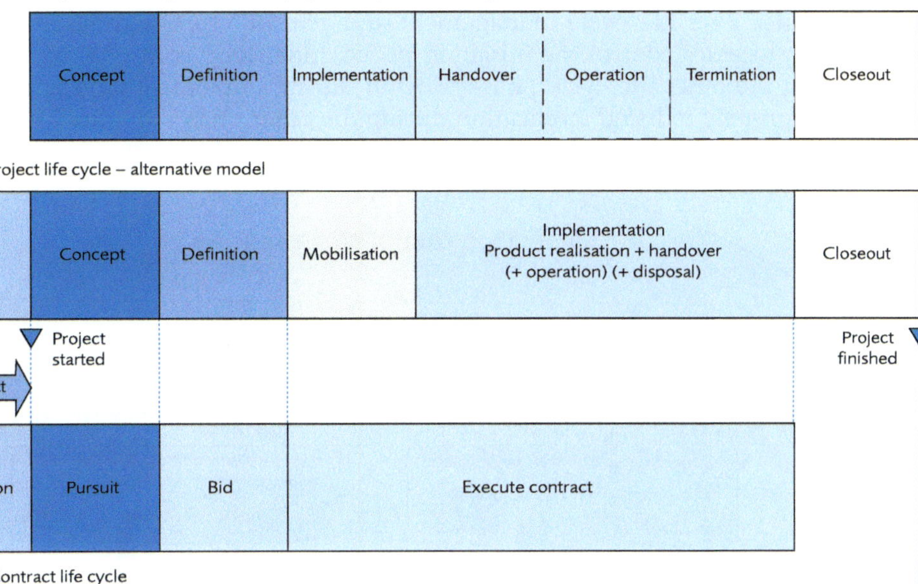

Figure 6: Project life cycle models

Where an organisation is undertaking projects for clients, and probably having to obtain contracts for those projects by competitive tendering, the project life cycle runs in parallel with a contract life cycle. In the contract life cycle an opportunity is first identified, then pursued and bid for; if the bid is successful a contract is then executed (Figure 6C). Organisations must generally spend internal contract acquisition funds ('marketing' and 'bidding' funds) on identification, pursuits and bids. If a contract is obtained at the end of a successful bid, the beginning of project mobilisation generally marks the transition from the use of internal funds to the use of external funds provided under the contract. After deductions for business costs (such as future marketing and bidding) and profit, the contract funding provides the project budget, which covers the costs of the project's mobilisation, implementation and closeout phases.

4.2 CONTROL ACTIVITIES IN EACH PHASE

The outer loop control processes wrap around all projects and operate for as long as an organisation is undertaking projects. The inner loop control processes reside within individual projects but apply selectively in different phases of the project life cycle. Project control is fully applied during the implementation phase, which is usually the longest and most costly phase of a project. The initiation phase is pre-project, so there's no inner loop control; the outer loop life cycle management and portfolio/programme management processes control the initiation phase. Inner loop control is necessary during the other life cycle phases, in full during implementation and with appropriately reduced application during the other phases (Figure 7).

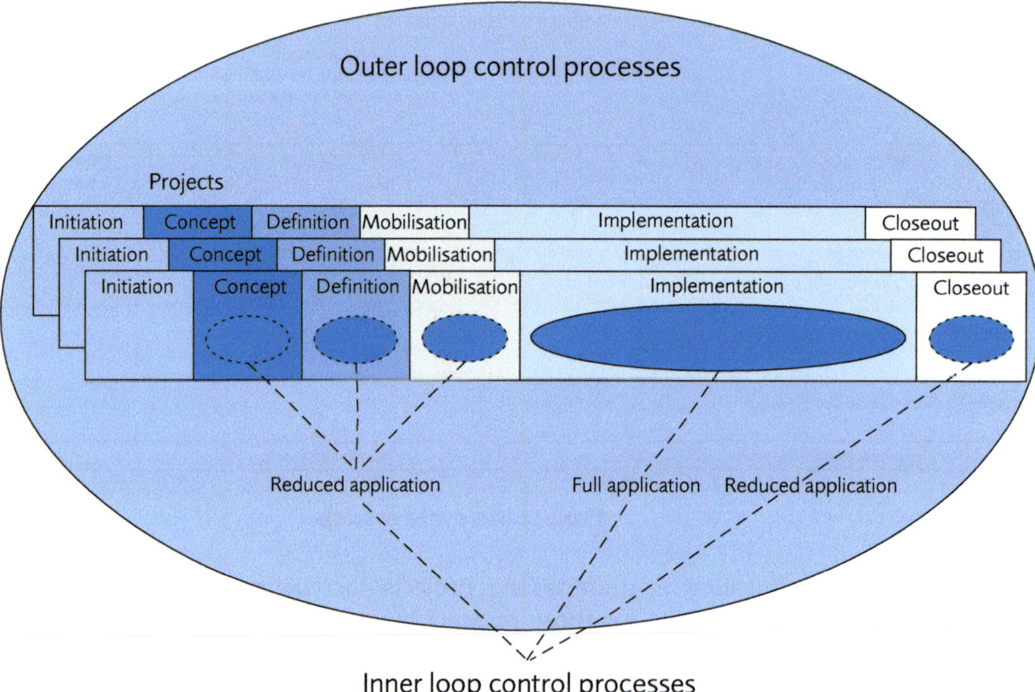

Figure 7: Application of control processes

4.2.1 Initiation phase

Initiation is a generally short pre-project phase which enables the organisation to confirm the need for a project. The need may arise either:

- within the organisation: as a result of a need for change, perhaps as part of a programme; or
- externally: through the identification of a potential business opportunity.

The need is concisely set out in a project initiation document or project brief, which is prepared by the sponsor, the programme management organisation or a marketing executive. The project initiation document is reviewed by the organisation at a life cycle management gate review. If this initiation review confirms the need for a project, a project manager is assigned with suitable terms of reference and a preliminary budget for the resources (personnel, facilities, time) required for the concept phase; the project starts. Alternatively, the initiation review may determine that no project is justified: the initiation phase enables considered no-project decisions to be made with minimal investment of time, effort and money.

4.2.2 Concept phase

During the concept phase, the need, opportunity or problem is confirmed, the feasibility of the project is considered and a preferred solution is identified. If the project is a potential external contract, the concept phase is informed by additional market intelligence obtained by the contract acquisition process. This helps to determine whether the organisation should continue to pursue the opportunity. The emphasis is on the strategic planning of the project; only limited consideration of the control processes to be used during implementation is generally necessary in the concept phase.

The project activities taking place in the concept phase may themselves require the application of project controls. For a simple project, the concept phase will itself be simple and limited in scope and time. Simple controls will be appropriate, such as maintenance of a schedule for the concept phase and monitoring of expenditure against the concept phase budget. Very large projects generally require extended concept phases, potentially incurring a small percentage of the overall expenditure of the entire project. In such cases the concept phase becomes a mini-project in its own right and more extensive application of project controls is appropriate.

The life cycle management gate review at the end of the concept phase tests the feasibility of the project and the soundness of its business case. The outline considerations of the control processes to be used during implementation will form only a small element of the review. Satisfactory completion of the review enables the project to continue into definition and where an external contract is being pursued, confirms the organisation's intention to bid.

4.2.3 Definition phase

During this phase, the preferred solution is further evaluated and optimised – often an iterative process. Where the potential project requires a competitive tender, the definition phase includes the preparation of the bid. There is a transition from strategic to detailed planning. The planning must consider how the organisation's standard project control processes need to be tailored to suit the specific needs of *this* project. Tailoring may need to be extensive if the project contains novel elements, or if the client imposes particular control requirements, such as specific reporting requirements. The non-recurring activities required to tailor the control processes must be included in the project's scope of work, unless the organisation determines that the changes will be of wider benefit and decides that a business investment should be made.

The recurring activities necessary to implement the controls are part of the project's scope of work and should be included in the work breakdown structure. The boundary between control activities to be undertaken as part of the project and the support to those activities given to the project by the business needs to be determined. Resources necessary to implement the activities within the project need to be included in the project's resource plan and cost estimate; support provided by the business is an overhead cost shared by all projects.

The amount of work necessary in the definition phase is typically several times greater than in the concept phase and the need for control is commensurately higher. Control of schedule and cost will certainly be required. The scope of the definition phase of a very large project may well match the scope of implementation phases of smaller projects and anything up to a complete implementation of project control processes may be necessary.

The gate review at the end of the definition phase tests that the project is satisfactorily planned; the existence of a sound and detailed plan is confirmation of the project's feasibility and the cost estimate contained in the plan is a central element of the refined business case. The definition of the control arrangements within the plan should be scrutinised during the review. A satisfactory review authorises an internal project to continue via mobilisation into implementation, or approves the submission of a tender for an external contract. In the latter case, continuation of the project depends on the success of the bid and on the acceptability of the contract offered by the client.

4.2.4 Mobilisation phase

The mobilisation phase is a relatively short, transitional phase between definition and implementation, during which the project team is brought together, equipment and facilities are secured, the plan is baselined and the initial implementation phase work packages are authorised. At the end of the mobilisation phase the project can be regarded as 'launched'.

The nucleus of the project team is likely to be the personnel who worked on the project during its concept and definition phases and who are already familiar with the project management plan. The project manager for concept and definition may continue to manage the project through mobilisation into implementation, or there may be a handover between managers who specialise in different project phases. New personnel must be inducted into the project team and the plan is formally communicated to the project team and key stakeholders, especially to those not involved in the definition phase.

The amount of time and effort required to mobilise depends on the project: larger and more complex projects have larger and more complex mobilisations, especially when a large project team is involved. A complex mobilisation should be specifically addressed in the project management plan.

The project control processes defined in the project management plan are established during mobilisation and begin to operate. Using the change management process, the plan is baselined as the basis for performance management and initial work packages are authorised. Risk management commences and the risk register becomes active, usually pre-populated with the project risks identified during definition. An issue log is established. If the mobilisation process spans more than a single review period, the review process commences. For large projects using earned value management, an integrated baseline review (IBR) may be performed. An IBR confirms that the plan is correct and comprehensive and is being implemented by the project team. An IBR may be a client requirement and is an early and robust demonstration that satisfactory project control is in place, but it is a prerequisite that at least one review cycle is completed before an IBR. If mobilisation is short, the IBR will therefore occur early in the implementation phase.

It is good practice to formalise the completion of mobilisation as part of the life cycle management process. The project manager must complete a mobilisation review with the sponsor and project board to satisfy them that the project is satisfactorily underway. A quick and effective mobilisation provides the best basis for the implementation phase, which is the main phase of the project.

4.2.5 Implementation phase

In the implementation phase, the project management plan is executed. As a minimum, implementation almost inevitably includes stages to realise the products (requiring design, build, integration, testing, etc.) and to hand them over to their users (requiring familiarisation and training). The scope of the project may also include technical and logistical support during an initial period of operation (the operation stage). The project may be extended to include subsequent periods of contractor support and possibly even to include the decommissioning and disposal of products at the end of their operational life (the disposal stage).

The plan defines how the project, including its control processes, should be implemented. Having mobilised, the control processes are fully operational and continue until the closeout phase. The plan in its initial form will almost certainly need to evolve during the implementation of the project, and so implementation includes:

- **Maintenance of the plan:** definition and implementation of routine changes to the plan, via change management, to address minor variances.
- **Re-planning:** definition and implementation of changes to the plan, again via change management, either within the existing scope (e.g. in response to critical variances) or with changes to scope (e.g. in response to client-requested changes).

On larger projects and projects with a long duration, organisations may operate rolling wave planning. Only the next stage of the implementation, or the next time window, is planned in great enough detail for control purposes. The next stage/time window must be planned in greater detail and baselined prior to implementation using the change control process; new work packages are authorised.

4.2.6 Closeout phase

Closeout is another relatively short phase, during which project matters are finalised, final project reviews are carried out, project information is archived and the project team is redeployed. Confirmation is sought that the project's objectives have been achieved and that all products/deliverables have been handed over to their users. Project expenditure is accounted for, and it is apparent whether the project has been completed within budget.

The valuable lessons accumulated by the end of a project should add to the organisation's project knowledge base to assist in planning successor projects. Many of the lessons will be implicit in the maintained plan, which at the end of the project will define exactly how implementation was carried out, and also in project reports. The reports may contain information on variances and their causes: the causes can be identified as threats to successor projects and perhaps eliminated during planning. Variances may require adjustments to organisational norms used in estimating, or to the organisation's processes. The completed risk register will identify threats and opportunities to be considered during the concept and definition phases of later projects, and the issues log may show that changes are necessary to the organisation's infrastructure and supporting processes.

4.3 CONTROL LEVERAGE ON PROJECT SUCCESS

The relative importance of the inner and outer loop control processes, the effort expended on them and, particularly, their leverage on the successful outcome of a project vary throughout the life cycle (Figure 8).

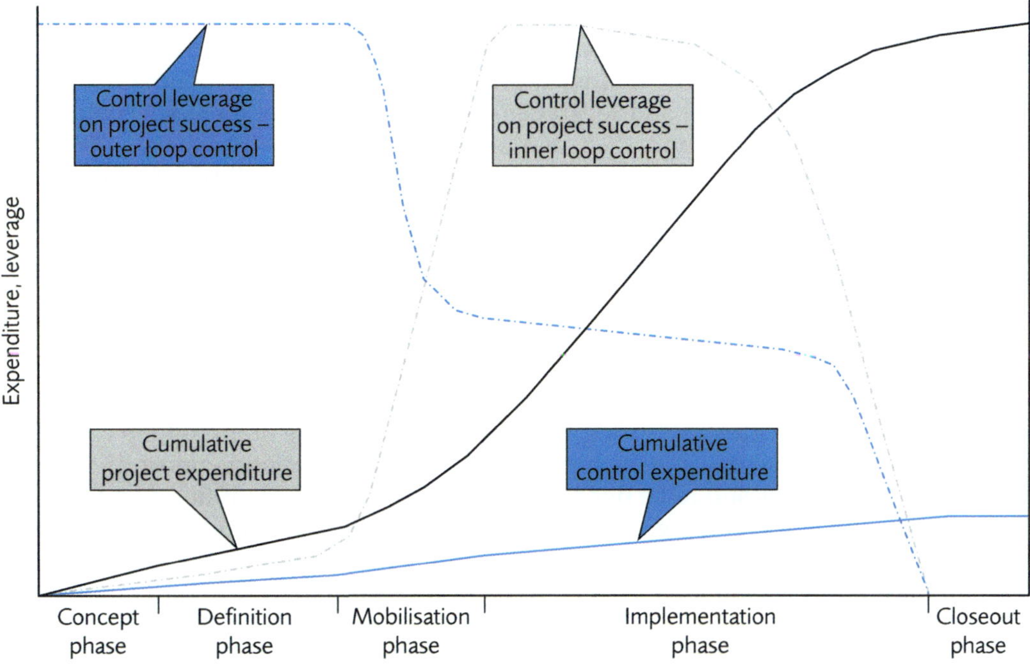

Figure 8: Control leverage on project success

4.3.1 Leverage of outer loop control

Pre-project, life cycle management and portfolio/programme management ensure that only potentially viable projects are started. After a project starts, these two outer loop control processes are at their most effective during the concept and definition phases, in ensuring that only well-planned projects with sound business cases are allowed to continue (i.e. 'the right projects'). Continuous improvement should ensure that lessons learned from predecessor projects are included in the project management plan and quality assurance should ensure that project quality planning is satisfactory.

The leverage of outer loop control begins to decline as mobilisation is successfully completed, during which phase inner loop control is becoming more significant. Programme management attends to interdependencies between related projects. Quality assurance and life cycle management continue for the remainder of the project. Continuous improvement may enable improvements during implementation, but the focus changes to capturing lessons learned to improve successor projects.

4.3.2 Leverage of inner loop control

Concept phases have relatively small scopes of work and are relatively informal; there is therefore only limited application of and leverage for inner loop control. The application and leverage of inner loop control increase gradually during definition and then markedly during the mobilisation, when extensive non-recurring effort is required to establish the full set of control processes ready for the implementation phase. The leverage that inner loop control has on the potential for project success greatly increases during mobilisation; a well-controlled and quick mobilisation ensures that implementation commences well.

At the end of mobilisation, the inner loop control processes should be fully operational and continue throughout the implementation phase. Expenditure on project control as a proportion of overall project expenditure is therefore at its greatest during this phase. The leverage of inner loop control on project success is at its highest early in implementation; most of the scope of work has still to be done and if variances can be identified and corrected early, there is the greatest potential to avoid impact on the project's objectives. The leverage declines as more of the scope of work is completed and less scope remains to correct variances without impact on project quality, time or cost.

During closeout, there is a limited amount of additional control effort involved in the preparation of final reports and in conducting final reviews. These have no further bearing on the success of the project, but are a necessary part of closeout contributing via continuous improvement to successor projects.

5
Who controls?

The project manager is, of course, the key figure in project control, and the bulk of the control work is performed by the project team. However, effective control engages all stakeholders in the project.

Figure 9 shows a generic project organisation for a project being performed for an external client. The project team consists of the project manager, project support experts, control account managers, other project team members and subcontractors. The project manager reports to the sponsor, who chairs the project board; the sponsor and the other project board members are either among the organisation's senior managers or they report to them. Some of the senior managers (project board members and others) are usually heads of the functions which perform work on behalf of the project team and/or second personnel into it. The project manager is the first point of contact for the client, and interfaces with any other external stakeholders.

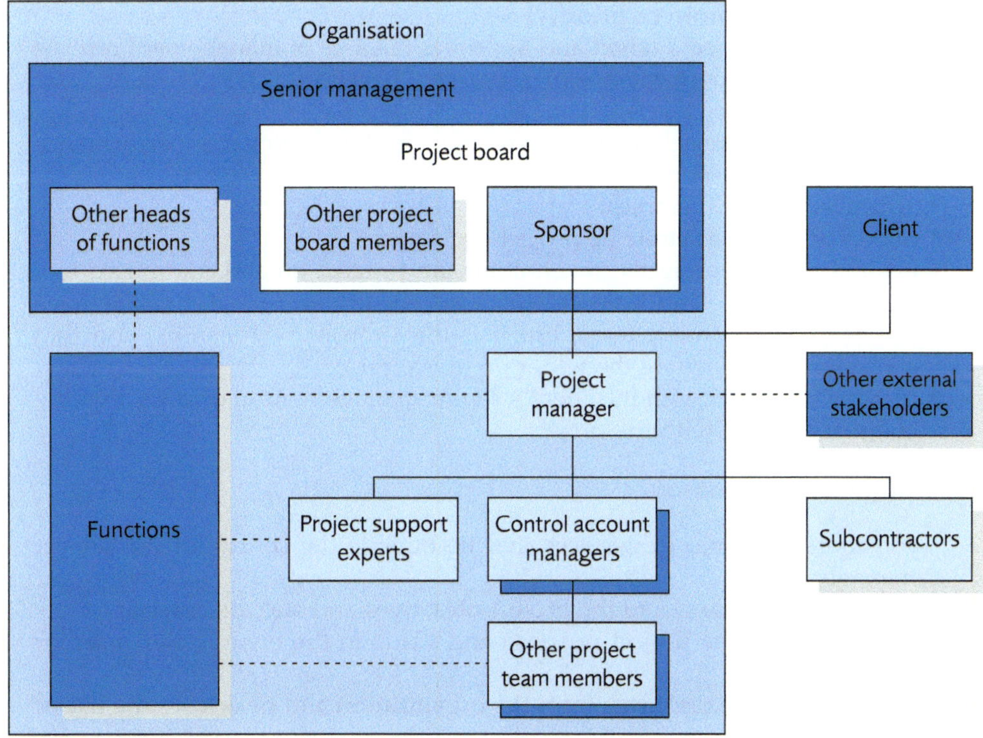

Figure 9: A generic project organisation

5.1 SPONSOR

Effective control begins with the project sponsor, because the sponsor determines the environment for projects and sets the standards for control. Without the interest of the sponsor in the outcomes of the control processes, control is unlikely to be accorded sufficient attention by the project manager and the project team. Therefore the sponsor needs to:

- establish and effectively chair the project board;
- set a high standard for reviews;
- understand the project and know what good performance looks like, for example being able to interpret the project's EVM reports;
- champion risk management and ensure that it achieves sufficient attention;
- ensure that issues can be raised without recrimination, and ensure that the necessary external support is provided to the project team when issues are raised.

Along with the project board, the sponsor:

- determines the project's priority;
- provides the project budget and approves releases of management reserve budget into the performance measurement baseline;
- approves resource levels;
- approves the project management plan and the project's performance measurement baseline;
- approves key deliverables;
- makes or endorses strategic project decisions;
- ensures that the project's stakeholders are focused on and committed to a common purpose and vision of success. (The project manager can achieve this within the project team, but it is the sponsor who can expand that commitment to include the wider organisation.);
- maintains contact with the client's senior management to confirm that the client is satisfied with the project.

In addition, the sponsor:

- considers the project interfaces that lie outside the control of the project manager;
- approves any changes to the project objectives and success criteria;
- communicates the project purpose and value to the organisation's senior management;
- commits specific resources from the organisation and prioritises the use of shared resources;
- paves the way for change in the affected organisational units.

The sponsor is likely to be, or have been, a senior and successful project manager and is likely to represent the organisation's project management function. Good sponsorship is hugely important for effective control and is necessary for good governance of project management. The nature of sponsorship is addressed in detail in the APM publication *Sponsoring Change: A Guide to the Governance Aspects of Project Sponsorship.*[3]

5.2 PROJECT BOARD

The project board is a steering group for one or more projects whose remit is to set the strategic direction for the project(s) and to provide guidance to the sponsor and the project manager. The project board represents the interests of the organisation, and assists the sponsor in assuring that the project is satisfactorily performed. Usually chaired by the sponsor, the project board includes other senior managers from the organisation: these should include senior representatives of the functions whose resources are performing the work (e.g. engineering, procurement, manufacturing, quality, etc.) and of supporting functions (e.g. compliance, commercial, finance, etc.). The senior functional managers are able to provide challenge, guidance and assistance based on extensive subject matter expertise, and to assist where the project team interacts with functional boundaries.

Along with the sponsor, the project board is centrally involved in the outer loop control processes, overseeing their operation, receiving reports and acting on them. So, for example, the project board receives the results and recommendations of life cycle management reviews and determines the appropriate outcome. The project board ensures the effective governance of its project(s).

5.3 PROJECT MANAGER

The project manager's role is to execute the project in accordance with the plan, controlling it effectively throughout using formal and informal control processes. The project manager:

- leads the project team;
- must appraise the sponsor of progress, seeking at all times to avoid surprises and as necessary, escalate issues to the sponsor;
- works with the functions performing project work and obtains suitably qualified and experienced personnel to be seconded into the project team;
- manages the relationship with the client;
- is the principal point of contact for other external stakeholders;

[3] Association for Project Management (2009) *Sponsoring Change: A Guide to the Governance Aspects of Project Sponsorship*, APM Knowledge, ISBN: 978-1-903494-30-1

- is responsible for the deployment of effective control processes by his team and for control interfaces with key stakeholders;
- must drive the inner loop control processes;
- must engage (and ensure that the rest of the project team engages) effectively with the outer loop processes, e.g. according high priority to life cycle management and quality assurance reviews.

5.4 PROJECT SUPPORT EXPERTS

On smaller projects, the project manager may personally operate the control processes: on larger projects, the project manager is likely to delegate this to project support experts. These are individuals with expertise in particular aspects of project planning and control, such as scheduling, budgeting, cost control, earned value management and reporting, and possibly risk management. 'Project support experts' have a range of different titles in different organisations, such as project controller, project coordinator, project planner, project support officer and scheduler.

Project support experts reside in and may be seconded into a project team from a project office. Project offices are likely to exist in organisations undertaking a lot of projects and are organisational groupings of functional specialists serving an organisation's project management needs. 'Project office' is a generic term covering a variety of different types of organisational groups providing a range of services, from supporting project managers to responsibility for linking an organisation's strategy to its project execution. For example, a programme management office (PMO) is responsible for the business and technical management of a programme: a PMO includes project support experts and deploys them across the programme's constituent projects.

Project support experts:

- implement the organisation's standard control processes (thereby fulfilling governance requirements), with the allowed tailoring to meet the project's unique needs as agreed in the project management plan;
- are central to performance control, being the personnel who measure or obtain the measurements of performance (quality, time, cost), analyse variances and run down and address some of the causes of variances, e.g. misbookings;
- lead the project team's application of the software tools and techniques which are likely to be used for inner loop control. In particular, project support experts are usually the principle users of scheduling software;
- devise and prepare individual metrics and compile reports for use in reviews;
- act as the conscience of the organisation, ensuring that the control processes are adhered to and that the status of the project is fairly and accurately presented.

Thus, project support experts free up project managers to perform higher-level management functions. They bring valuable experience of previous projects and the lessons learned from them and hence cannot only directly influence how the project will be implemented, but can help ensure its viability. Project support expertise can make a huge difference to projects, especially in support of novice project managers and in newly-formed project teams, as well as on complex projects. Project support experts help a project team a bit like stabilisers help a novice cyclist control a bike.

5.5 CONTROL ACCOUNT MANAGERS

On larger projects, the project manager may delegate to other managers the responsibility for implementation of elements of the overall scope of work. These managers then 'own' and must deliver specific elements of the work breakdown structure (WBS). Various different terms are used to describe the project roles of such managers, including work package manager and WBS element owner, or in organisations implementing earned value management, control account manager (CAM). Each CAM is accountable for one or more control accounts, each control account being a defined subset of a project's scope of work, usually a set of related work packages. CAMs are responsible for ensuring that their control account is completed to time and to budget, with products/deliverables meeting their quality requirements. They are responsible for the development, execution, and control of their work scope within the schedule. Each manages the control account as a contract between with the project manager and interfaces the work of the project with the work of one of the organisation's functions.

Delegation to CAMs should be based on their functional skills and experience and also on their interest in and aptitude for managing the work, i.e. CAMs should have some project management ability. CAMs should be involved in project planning, where their subject matter expertise improves the quality of the plan. Especially with foreknowledge of the plan, they achieve ownership of their control accounts and are ready to hit the ground running when implementation starts. Their combination of subject matter expertise and project management ability ideally suits them to controlling work with a significant functional or discipline-specific content.

The involvement of CAMs in project control is a subset of the project manager's role. Each control account is effectively a mini-project to be delivered, but must be integrated into the overall project through consideration of logical links and interdependencies with other control accounts.

5.6 OTHER PROJECT TEAM MEMBERS

The role of other project team members seconded into the project team from the organisation's functions is to ensure that their functional skills and experience contribute to effective control. While seeking to perform their individual activities to schedule and with attention to cost, they should particularly ensure that the quality requirements relevant to their function or discipline are achieved. In addition, all team members should:

- support performance measurement, e.g. advising on the progress of their activities when the project schedule is updated;
- ensure that costs are collected accurately. For example, time worked booked to the appropriate work packages; purchase orders raised against and invoiced to the correct work packages;
- contribute to estimates to complete;
- identify risks, help to assess them and accept assignments as risk owners and risk action owners as part of the required risk responses;
- promptly identify problems to the control account manager or project manager.

In addition, each team member should apply functional expertise. For example:

- Engineers should ensure that the project is implemented using a rigorous engineering process that should have been defined in the PMP: design stages should be evident in the WBS and schedule and product realisation reviews should be apparent as key milestones. Engineering activities in general and product realisation reviews in particular should be conducted in accordance with the organisation's engineering processes.
- Procurement specialists should implement the overall procurement strategy and individual subcontract strategies defined in the PMP, enabling subcontractors to contribute effectively to the project.
- Manufacturing specialists should have ensured that manufacturing set up and low-rate initial production are included in the PMP as required and that production schedules and cost estimates are based on relevant norms for the organisation. They should ensure that manufacturing elements of the project are delivered in accordance with the plan, resolving potential conflicts within the manufacturing function between projects and business as usual.
- Commercial specialists should satisfy themselves that the client's contractual requirements are being satisfied, that contracted deliverables remain aligned with the customer's requirements and that progress payments are invoiced.

5.7 SUBCONTRACTORS

Subcontractors provide goods, services, data or other products/deliverables to the organisation for use in the project. Suppliers provide resources; the distinction is that these resources are available off the shelf as commodities, requiring straightforward procurement action by the organisation. On the other hand, subcontractors must perform parts of the project's scope of work and are performing a project on behalf of the contractor organisation which is their client.

Subcontractors should have been chosen, *inter alia*, for the effectiveness of their own project control processes. They should contribute effectively to the contractor organisation's project with on-time delivery of products/ deliverables meeting the necessary quality standards. In particular, they should:

- work closely with the project manager, control account managers and other points of contact in the contractor organisation: there should be sharp focus on interdependencies and surprises should be avoided;
- ensure that their schedule dovetails with the project master schedule;
- highlight key risks and escalate issues to the project manager, in the same way that the project manager escalates issues to the sponsor.

Subcontractors' performance is vital to the success of the project so subcontractors should be treated and should behave as members of the project team: the contractor's and subcontractors' project control processes must integrate to enable this to happen.

5.8 FUNCTIONS

Organisations usually contain functions containing specialist resources performing a particular role, e.g. marketing, project management, engineering, procurement, manufacturing, quality, compliance, commercial, finance, information technology, legal, human resources. Projects cannot be conducted without the functions' resources and without the infrastructure of business processes that they operate. Some functions (e.g. engineering, procurement) may second personnel to work inside a project team: this usually happens where individuals are going to be almost solely focused on an individual project for a significant time period. Other functions (finance, legal, human resources) may be needed only occasionally, or may be supporting multiple projects each on a part-time basis: personnel from such functions are generally not seconded into project teams and remain in their functional bases. Functional resources may be direct costs to the project, or may be indirect costs shared among projects via overhead costs.

The contribution of functional personnel to project control is like that of other project team members (Section 5.6), except that they are likely to have to contribute simultaneously to multiple projects while also contributing to business as usual.

5.9 CLIENT

The client organisation needs to assure itself that its project, being performed by a contractor organisation, remains on plan. It is likely to have appointed its own project manager to oversee one or more contracted projects and report to a sponsor in the client organisation. The client's project manager is likely to be the principal point of contact with the contractor's project manager and a close and effective working relationship between these two project managers, who have a shared interest in the project's success, is conducive to achieving the project's objectives.

The client, via its project manager:

- should fulfil its obligations to its contractor, such as timely fulfilment of dependencies such as provision of client-furnished equipment (CFE);
- may have specified particular project control arrangements and must assure itself in day-to-day contact and formal reviews that these are being adhered to;
- should receive regular reports and hold regular progress reviews. Reviews should cover the project's quality, time and cost dimensions as well as key risks and any issues. The client should enforce high standards for reports and reviews;
- should respond to any issues raised by the contractor;
- should participate in the change management process, originating external change requests and responding to change requests from the contractor. Both parties should endeavour to minimise such changes.

Overall, the client's role is somewhat akin to that of the sponsor; by being interested in and setting high but realistic expectations for control, it reinforces the contractor's efforts to achieve effective control.

5.10 OTHER EXTERNAL STAKEHOLDERS

In addition to a client and subcontractors, there may be other project stakeholders external to the organisation involved in project control. There are too many potential external stakeholders and too many potential interactions to cover here, but the following are a couple of examples:

- Airworthiness authorities are involved in aerospace projects.
- Nuclear regulators are involved in projects in the nuclear industry.

Such stakeholders must be involved in quality control, review and quality assurance to ensure that the necessary standards are being achieved and to enable products to be granted any necessary certification.

6
How to control?

6.1 PERFORMING THE WORK – A GENERIC PROJECT

The control processes wrap around the core work of a project and must suit the needs of that work. However, it's helpful in introducing project control to consider the work of a generic project to help illustrate how control operates. Figure 10 therefore represents the work of a generic project during its implementation phase, focussing on the product realisation stage. The scope of supply of this generic project is a new system - an integrated set of products which function together to provide a new capability addressing a new set of user needs. The scope of work of the product realisation stage is the core work involved in realising the new system, ready for handover, plus the associated work of project control. In practice, the user needs will already have had some analysis: draft user requirements will already have been captured and conceptual design work carried out during the concept and definition phases, to identify the system solution, assess feasibility and to enable the project to be planned.

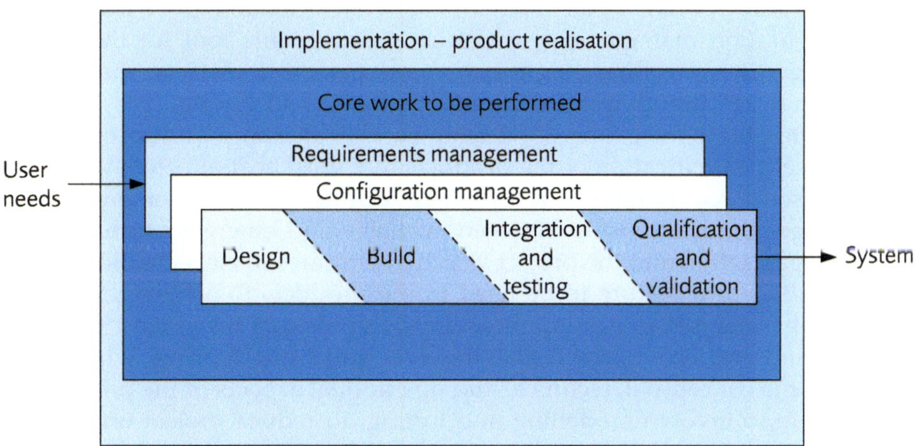

Figure 10: Core work of a generic project

The core work of product realisation is:

a) **Requirements management.** This is the process of capturing the user needs, analysing and testing them to create a documented statement of user requirements. The requirements should be comprehensive, clear, well structured, traceable and testable, and should include acceptance criteria. A clear and agreed expression of requirements and their acceptance criteria is essential for project success as it manages stakeholder expectations and provides a measure against which project success can be judged. The requirements should be reviewed with and agreed by the users. The agreed requirements are the baseline for configuration management of the products and for change management of the project: changes to user requirements during project implementation are one of the greatest challenges for scope and change management, uncontrolled requirements change being a principal cause of scope creep and a common reason for project failure. For all but the simplest projects, requirements management is likely to involve specialist personnel using specialist software tools to create and maintain a database of requirements, which should be populated progressively with the evidence that their acceptance criteria are being achieved.

b) **Configuration management.** A configuration is a definition of the functional and physical characteristics of a product. Configuration management is the set of technical and administrative activities concerned with the creation, maintenance and controlled change of the configuration throughout this project life cycle. At the end of the product realisation stage, the configuration of the products should satisfy the user requirements and the requirements database should contain the evidence that they do so. Specialist personnel and software are likely to be involved in configuration management, which is an invaluable tool for the project manager in controlling the project's products, particularly as they evolve and mature through design, build, integration and testing.

c) **Design.** This is the process of defining and evaluating product options to arrive at a specification of the products that most cost-effectively satisfies the user's requirements. It involves technology management, which manages the relationship between available and emerging technologies, the organisation and the project which determines those technologies that are sufficiently mature to be used in the products to achieve functional and physical advantages without excessive risk to the project's quality, time and cost objectives. It also involves value engineering, which optimises the conceptual, technical and operational aspects of the products. It is likely to involve modelling and testing, to reduce project uncertainty and risk by providing early assurance that the emerging design will satisfy the user requirements. The design process involves specialists from the appropriate engineering disciplines and their specialist processes and software tools; the specialists are either seconded into the project team or remain in their functional departments, with which the project manager must interface. The system of products is likely to contain a number of subsystems, which themselves consist of components, which are the lowest-level elements of the system. The design process captures the user requirements (via requirements management), defines requirements for a system that will meet the user requirements and designs the system, its subsystems and components. Each level of design generates the requirements for the next-level elements of the system, and defines the interfaces between those elements. Ultimately, the requirements for system components are sufficiently detailed for the design of those components to commence. Design, build and test of subsystems or components may be performed in house or subcontracted.

d) **Build.** This is the creation of the lowest-level components of the system, involving their final, detailed design and the building and testing of prototypes and preproduction examples. Low rate and volume production, after qualification and validation, may bc part of project or may be business as usual activities. Procurement is centrally involved, this being the process by which the resources (goods and services) required by the project are acquired. In the generic project, there are procurements both of components for subsystems being developed in house and of entire subsystems. The project team must employ effective procurement techniques to ensure that the procured components and subsystems are of the required quality and are delivered on time and to cost. Procurements must be in accordance with the project's procurement strategy, which will reflect the organisation's overall procurement strategy with regard to key technologies which must remain in house and with regard to strategic relationships with key subcontractors and suppliers. Components and subsystems must be progressively and iteratively worked up in house and by subcontractors (development) and must be accompanied by supporting evidence that they satisfy their requirements. This evidence contributes to the overall body of evidence that ultimately demonstrates that overall system quality/acceptance criteria have been achieved.

e) **Integration and testing.** This is the bringing together of the subsystems, to confirm that they work as an integrated system to deliver the required functionality and performance. Each level of integration is accompanied by testing to verify that the integrated components, subsystems or system satisfy their requirements. Integration and testing are usually progressive, in terms of both scope and maturity, and a philosophy of 'build a bit, test a bit' is the best way to manage complexity and progressively eliminate risk. In terms of scope, integration and testing usually commence with a core system to which additional subsystems are progressively added. In terms of maturity, integration and testing usually commence with prototype or preproduction subsystems with limited functionality and performance. Integration and testing is therefore iterative and presents significant project management challenges; configuration management keeps track of the status of the products and requirements management keeps track of the acceptance evidence generated by testing.

f) **Qualification and validation.** Qualification demonstrates that the project's products meet the necessary technical standards, including any external standards such as those for airworthiness or nuclear safety. Validation demonstrates that the products fulfil the user's needs, usually involving trials by user representatives. Qualification and validation may require dedicated testing (including user trials), but risk is better managed and the extent of additional testing is minimised, if as much as possible of the evidence required is generated progressively during design, build, integration and testing. Any system changes shown to be necessary during qualification and validation will require re-design, additional development, additional integration and testing and repetition of the relevant qualification and validation activities. Changes identified so late in product realisation are likely to have a disastrous impact on project time and cost, unless it is possible to negotiate some relaxation of the affected user requirements. It is much better to identify the need for change earlier.

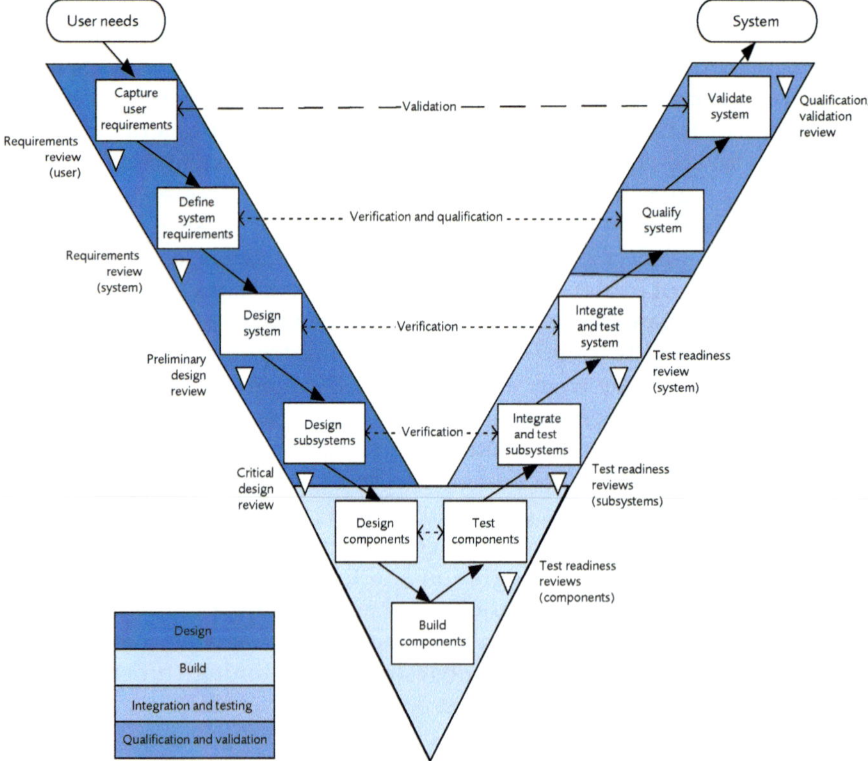

Figure 11: Product realisation – the 'V model'

The work of product realisation can be represented in a "V model" (Figure 11). This illustrates the verification and validation of components, subsystems and the system against their respective requirements. The tasks shown in the V are a good basis for the work breakdown structure of the project, defining logical work packages. Towards the bottom of the V, the WBS fans out as subsystem and component work packages proceed in parallel, and then fans in again up the right-hand side of the V as components, subsystems and the system are integrated. The schedule for such a project, in Gantt chart form, resembles a waterfall.

Figure 11 indicates the positioning of product realisation reviews: these are a key part of the quality control and review processes and are described in Section 6. Successful completion of each review is a significant project milestone.

6.2 INNER LOOP CONTROL PROCESSES

The inner loop control processes are represented in Figure 12. Together, they are a feedback control system for the project as defined during the definition phase and established during mobilisation. The management of performance, risk and issues provide feedback loops around the performance of the work; variances from the plan require responses which are implemented via change management. Figure 12 is schematic and highly simplified and as a consequence of this, the review process appears to have no specific connections to the other control processes. In practice, review relies on outputs from all of the other processes in order to synthesise a comprehensive and accurate view of the status of the project in order to inform the project manager, sponsor, project board and other stakeholders. Emerging from review may be requirements additional to the project.

6.2.1 Performance management

The performance management process is the innermost of the project's inner control loops, the process implemented at highest frequency and involving the most diverse set of techniques, both formal and informal. The essence of performance management is measurement of project activities, analysis of the performance revealed by the measurements and the identification of suitable responses to variances from plan revealed by the analysis (Figure 13). The scope of the performance being managed is all three dimensions of the project – quality, time and cost:

a) **Quality.** Quality control is part of overall project quality management which ensures that the both the products of the project and the processes by which the products are realised meet the needs of the stakeholders.

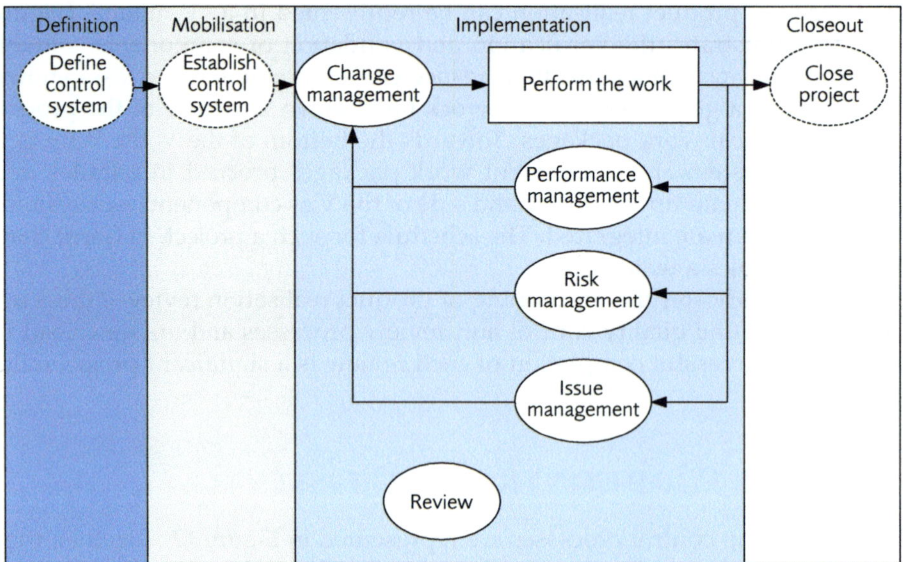

Figure 12: The inner loop control processes

'Quality' means not only the conformance of products and processes to specific requirements but also their fitness for purpose. Quality management consists of quality planning, quality control, quality assurance and continuous improvement. Quality planning is part of the overall project planning process and is carried out during the concept and definition phases; it influences the approach to the project, the scope of work and the processes to be used, to define how the quality-related objectives of the project will be met. Quality control verifies that the project's products conform to their requirements and are fit for purpose. This is achieved by inspection, testing and quality measurement. It is quality *control* rather than overall quality management which is carried out as part of the inner-loop performance management process, because quality planning precedes project implementation and quality assurance and continuous improvement are outer loop control processes. Quality assurance provides confidence to project stakeholders that the requirements for quality will be achieved and continuous improvement ensures that successive projects achieve their objectives more efficiently and effectively that their predecessors. These two processes are addressed in Section 6.5.

b) **Time.** Projects have a defined start and end and in between these points the products must be delivered when required by the users in order for the full benefits of the project to be realised. While the project objectives specify when the products must be handed over, it is necessary to focus on the timing of intermediate activities to ensure that the project will ultimately deliver its products at the required time. A better term for 'time control' is *scheduling*. During project planning, scheduling ensures that the activities constituting the project's scope of work are arranged in the optimum sequence. The activities, their durations and the start and finish dates defined by the logic network are shown in the project's schedule. During project implementation, adherence to the baseline schedule is monitored and deviations from it are addressed. Activities may need to be re-sequenced if predecessors are running late or if a required resource is unavailable. Particular attention should be paid to the critical path and opportunities to 'crunch' critical activities, to shorten them and the project overall, should be addressed. The time required to complete remaining work is closely examined when estimates to complete are carried out.

c) **Cost.** Project planning provides a cost estimate for a project. Funding is provided by the organisation or by the client via a contract and a project budget is established to cover the costs. A project budget includes a performance measurement baseline (PMB) budget to cover the cost of the defined scope of work, plus a management reserve budget to cover emergent costs. PMB budgets are sub-divided into budgets for particular elements of the overall scope of work, e.g. control accounts and their constituent work packages. Management reserve budgets generally include provisions for specific risks identified during planning, plus an additional non-specific risk provision to cover unforeseen arisings. Project cost control ensures costs are accurately collected, measures the accumulating actual cost of work packages and control accounts against their budgets, identifies variances and potential future overspends and applies corrective actions to minimise them.

The project manager and control account managers exercise informal management of quality, time and cost on an hour-by-hour basis throughout the project, based on their subjective assessment of the status of project activities. They employ knowledge and experience of the type of work being undertaken and are involved with other members of the project team throughout implementation, hence they should be able to identify and correct many potential performance issues almost as soon as they become apparent. Changes to address potential issues are likely to be informal and speedy, for example in the form of advice to a junior member of the project team about a better way of performing an activity.

Formal performance management uses techniques based on quantitative measures of performance and is undertaken at lower frequency, for example at the frequency of the review cycle or in response to a particular event in a project, such as completion of a particular test. The quantitative techniques include:

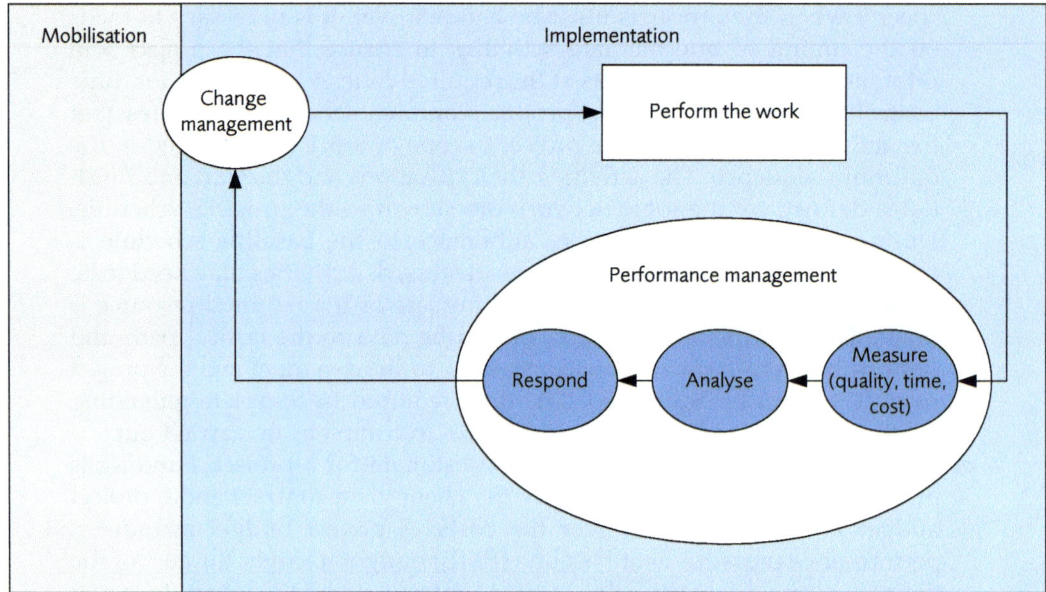

Figure 13: The performance management process

a) **Quality.** The statistical quality control techniques often applied to recurring processes in business as usual are generally not applicable to projects given the non-recurring nature of their activities. Progress towards the products' conformance to their requirements and fitness for purpose is progressive and involves inspection, testing and quality measurement of intermediate products at different levels of maturity (e.g. prototypes and pre-production versions) and of completeness (e.g. components and subsystems) as well as of the final products. Some of the quality control activities must happen at subcontractors' premises, enabled by appropriate subcontract terms and conditions, and facilitated by the subcontractor behaving as part of an extended project team. Quality requirements must be defined for the intermediate products and conformance verified in order to progressively retire technical risk from the project; waiting to test final products with the potential only then to reveal significant design deficiencies is a high risk strategy. So intermediate products must be inspected (e.g. is there sufficient access for maintenance?), tested (e.g. is it strong enough?) and measured (e.g. is it the right size?). The quantitative measures generally use pass/fail criteria or tolerances to confirm conformance to requirements. Inspection, testing and quality measurement are used to demonstrate conformance with essential technical standards (for qualification purposes). Validation testing such as user trials ultimately demonstrates fitness for purpose. Inspection, testing and quality measurement generate evidence to enable acceptance of the products. Smart project planning and control ensure that quality evidence for multiple purposes is generated without duplication of inspection, testing and measurement. It is often necessary to involve clients and users in witnessing quality control activities even on intermediate products such as subsystems and components; thus progressive acceptance of products is achieved.

b) **Time.** Scheduling naturally centres on the project schedule, which to be effective must include the planned (baseline) timing of activities and milestones and current information on their completion or forecast dates. In their scheduling role, project support experts work in the project team to keep the schedule up to date: the project manager must heed variances from the schedule and react accordingly. Responses to variances include re-sequencing work, assigning additional resources or even finding alternative methods of achieving the required outcomes. The integrated master schedule provides the definitive data on project timing, but generally is not suitable for all purposes. So, for example, identification of the critical path within the schedule, analyses of milestones and the charting of key milestone trends all focus attention on the most important timing elements. Higher-level summary schedules provide timing information in a form digestible by the project sponsor, the project board, clients and other stakeholders. Three point estimating of durations and Monte Carlo simulation of the project schedule to evaluate the probable range of outcomes, initially introduced on very large projects, are gradually flowing down to medium-sized projects, providing additional insight for the project manager.

c) **Cost.** Cost requires a sufficiently-accurate estimate of project cost, broken down to appropriately-low levels of the WBS, e.g. via control accounts to work packages. When work packages are authorised, budgets are assigned from PMB budget to cover the estimated costs. Cost control measures the costs actually incurred, responds to variances to budget and forecasts costs at completion for individual work packages and for the project as a whole. It is important to ensure that costs can be and are accurately collected against the work packages to which they relate – otherwise the analysis of cost performance is severely degraded. Forecasting includes both extrapolation and estimates to complete (ETCs). ETCs should be complied periodically by examination of the time and cost required to complete remaining work. The estimate of cost to complete is added to the actual cost of work performed (ACWP) to create an estimate at complete (EAC) which can be compared with the PMB budget. Cost control also involves the tracking and distribution of management reserve budget when required. Management reserve is 'owned' by the project sponsor rather than the project manager and transactions drawing down management reserve to increase the PMB budget should be subject to formal change control action. The project team should track cost commitments, for example incurred by letting subcontracts and cost accruals for work done with payment pending need to be taken into account when considering actual cost. The time-phased expenditure profile for the project (reflecting the cost of the individual activities at the times defined in the project schedule) is an important consideration for the organisation's cashflow: on projects for external clients, client payments need to be planned and achieved in order to obtain satisfactory cashflow. Tracking actual cost against the expenditure profile is a powerful technique but becomes even more powerful when the tracking also includes a third parameter, the value of the work completed: this is earned value management (EVM).

EVM is the single most powerful performance management technique. It determines:

- what of the planned work has been completed;
- what it has cost to complete this work;
- whether the work completed has cost more or less than planned;
- whether the project is ahead of or behind the planned schedule.

In doing this, EVM combines quantitative information about all three project dimensions, quality, cost and time, to determine how much of the plan has been achieved and how much that achievement has actually cost. The time and cost variances from plan identified by earned value analysis, the trends measured over time and the forecasts of time and money required to complete the project are pieces of vital information about the status of the project, they should prompt rapid and effective corrective action by the project manager, and should either comfort or alarm the project sponsor. EVM is addressed in the APM publication *Earned Value Management: APM Guidelines.*[4]

While quality, time and cost dimensions are all important parts of a project's objectives, in practice one or other dimension may assume greater importance at particular times during project implementation. In managing performance, the project manager may need to pragmatically trade among these dimensions in pursuit of the final objectives. So, for example, it may be necessary to accept a slightly lower degree of technical maturity (quality) in a prototype in order to utilise a narrow time window of availability of a key test facility.

[4] Association for Project Management (2002) *Earned Value Management: APM Guidelines*, APM Knowledge, ISBN: 978-1-903494-15-8

6.2.2 Risk management

As well as being inherently unstable, projects are inherently risky because they are unique, constrained, complex, based on assumptions and performed by people. Risk management should therefore continue throughout the project life cycle. It is predictive in that it addresses potential events (threats and opportunities) which may impact the project's objectives, but is closed loop in that it identifies and measures risks, determines appropriate responses to them and implements the responses. The alert project manager and project team will watch out for risks at all times. The formal, quantitative application of risk management during project implementation takes place at the review frequency of the project – typically monthly – enabling the risk status of the project to be presented in progress reviews.

For risk management to operate effectively, appropriate activity is necessary in each phase of the project. In the concept phase, this includes preliminary identification and assessment of risks so that they may be taken into consideration in determining the project's feasibility. More intensive risk management activities take place during the definition and mobilisation phases, with peak levels of risk management activity during implementation and follow-up work during closeout (Figure 14).

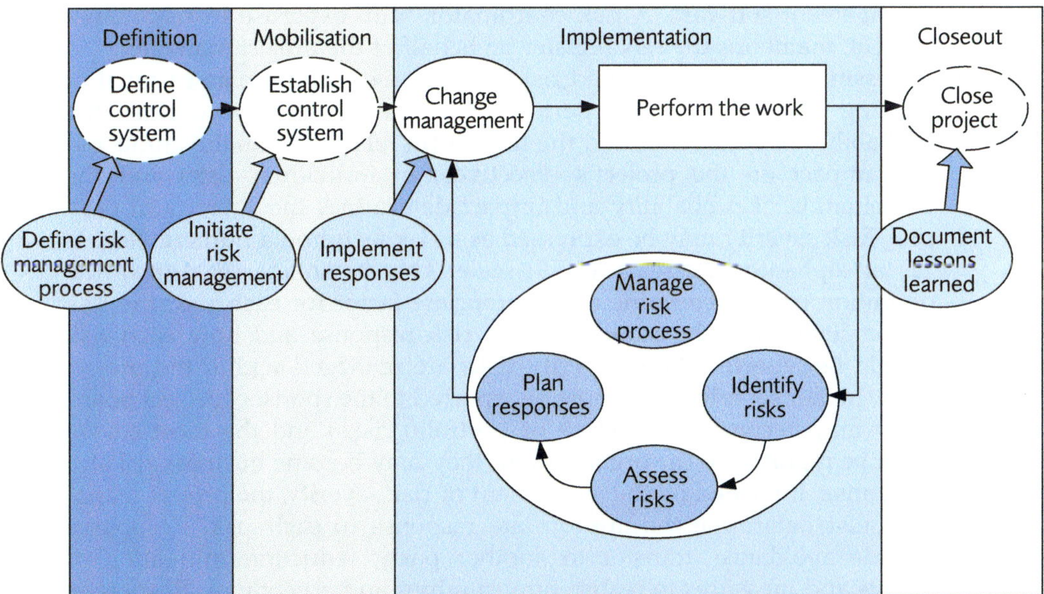

Figure 14: The risk management process

During definition, the risk management process that will be applied to the project is defined. Provision for its implementation must be included in the scope of work, resource plan and cost estimate. The process may be an organisational standard, with only minimal adjustment required to suit the project, such as the choice of threshold values of quality, time and cost impacts. In other cases, a client may specify a particular approach to risk management, including the choice of risk management software. During definition, the risk register should already be operational, enabling risks to be addressed while planning the project. Responses to them and appropriate contingency provisions should be included in the project management plan.

During mobilisation, risk management is formally initiated and this process will continue throughout implementation. The risk management process involves the following:

a) **The identification of risks.** Uncertain events are only risks to the project if they relate to the project's objectives. Anyone in or supporting the project team should be encouraged to identify risks at any time, but from time to time during the project's life cycle there should be specific team events to identify risks; these are usually called risk workshops and involve the brainstorming of uncertain events which might impact the objectives. Identified risks are documented in the risk register, which may be implemented as a simple spreadsheet or using sophisticated risk management software. A risk coordinator, with expertise in risk management, maintains the risk register on behalf of the project manager.
b) **Assessment.** Newly-identified risks are assessed, and the assessment of existing risks is updated periodically. The assessment defines the probability of occurrence and the impact (in relation to quality, time and cost impact on the project's objectives) of individual risks and the combination of probability and impact determines the severity of each risk. Risk severity may be expressed as a risk factor on a numeric (e.g. 1-12) or alphanumeric (e.g. A1-E5) scale. The thresholds set during the definition phase determine the appropriate factor for each risk; the risk factor determines the priority of the risk response and how each risk should be reported. Low severity risks are managed within the project team; higher severity risks must be reported to the sponsor/project board (they may become programme or portfolio risks) and the most severe must be reported to the organisation (they may become business risks).
c) **Response.** Informed by the assessment of risk severity, the project manager must determine the appropriate response to each risk. Responses include avoidance, transfer to another party, reduction/mitigation of threats and measures to realise opportunities and acceptance. Responses must be revisited from time to time as risk assessments change and as the date of the uncertain event draws closer. Definition of effective responses is central to effective risk management: see, for example the APM

publication *Prioritising Project Risks.*[5] Active responses to risks require changes to the way the project's work is being performed and hence changes to management action to ensure that the required changes occur.

Projects are dynamic and their risks continuously evolve so to be effective, the risk management process must operate continuously. There are synergistic control benefits when risk management is combined with earned value management; the former is forward looking while the latter measures performance and extrapolates forward. The APM publication *Interfacing Risk and Earned Value Management*[6] explains the synergies. Management of the risk process should ensure that comprehensive risk records are maintained, which should be reviewed and the lessons learned documented during project closeout. In doing this, threats can be planned out of successor projects and opportunities can be planned in.

The sponsor and project board should promote a culture in which risk management is important and where it responds positively when a project manager requests assistance in responding to risks, or when threats materialise in spite of effective management effort.

Risk management is addressed in the APM publication *Project Risk Analysis and Management Guide, 2nd edition.*[7]

6.2.3 Issue management

While risks are uncertain events that could potentially impact on project objectives, problems arise from events that have actually occurred; they are certain and present, i.e. a clear and present danger. Many problems are routine and can be resolved by the project manager and the project team, but a subset of problems (hopefully a minority) cannot be resolved in this way. The problems in this category are called issues, and issue management is the process by which such problems are identified and addressed. For example, a short-term absence due to illness of a member of the project team would not be a problem if another team member could temporarily undertake the activities without impact on the critical path; the illness would become a issue if it became protracted, started to impact the critical path and could not be addressed by re-assigning other members of the project team.

The significance of issues is that they cannot be resolved within the project; outside assistance must therefore be sought, requiring issues to be escalated. Issues are initially escalated to the project sponsor, who in turn may need to

[5] Association for Project Management (2008) *Prioritising Project Risks,* APM Knowledge, ISBN: 978-1-903494-27-1

[6] Association for Project Management (2008) *Interfacing Risk and Earned Value Management,* APM Knowledge, ISBN: 978-1-903494-24-0

[7] Association for Project Management (2004) *Project Risk Analysis and Management Guide, 2nd edition,* APM Knowledge, ISBN: 978-1-90-349412-7

escalate them to the project board. It is important that the project manager and his team solve routine problems themselves, so that only true issues are escalated. It is also important that the sponsor and the board operate a culture within which issues can be escalated without fear of blame or reprisal, and within which requests for assistance are positively received and promptly responded to. Prompt and effective responses to issues are characteristics of effective sponsors and project boards.

An issue log is used to track the progress of issues from identification to resolution. Maintained by the project manager or project support experts, the issues log describes each issue, who raised it, the date it was formally raised, possible consequences or impacts on the project, possible resolution and the resolution owner, the outcome and the date the issue is closed.

The quantity and severity of issues are a useful measurement of the state of the project and the completed issues log is a useful source of lessons learned material during project closeout.

6.2.4 Review

Review ensures that the status of the project is known to the project manager, the project team, the sponsor/project board and other stakeholders. Regular progress reviews provide a useful drumbeat for the project, ensuring that the inner control loops are operating effectively and sufficiently quickly. The project team knows that performance must be measured, analysed and responded to and actions completed in time for the next progress review. Review also includes event-driven reviews concerned with product realisation, earned value management and life cycle management. The latter relate to the outer loop life cycle management processes but are introduced here for completeness. The event-driven reviews are generally key project milestones, marking the achievement of a required level of process or technical maturity and the retirement of a significant amount of project risk. Some may be go/no go gates for continuation into later phases or stages of the project.

Figure 15 illustrates reviews for a generic project of the type described in section 6.1. The reviews include:

a) **Progress reviews.** These are calendar driven and occur at a frequency determined for the project, typically monthly and often synchronised with financial periods. The project manager presents the status of the project to the sponsor and the project board, covering performance (quality, time and cost) and risk, and identifying issues which require assistance from the sponsor/project board.
b) **Product realisation reviews.** Figure 11 indicated the positioning of these reviews on the product realisation V Model. They mark the completion of product realisation processes, demonstrating the increasing maturity of the products that the project is required to deliver. They demonstrate the quality of the products and progressively retire risks. A user requirement

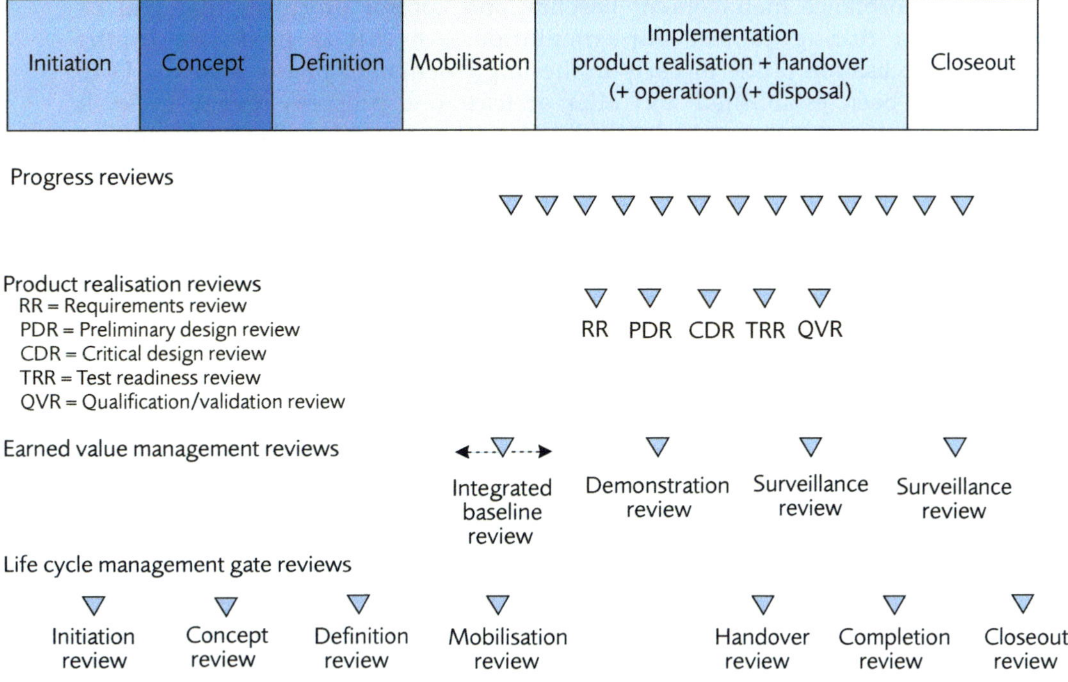

Figure 15: Reviews

review seeks to confirm that the user's requirements have been accurately and comprehensively captured, often in a user requirements document (URD). A system requirements review confirms the requirements for the system of products that will satisfy the customer's requirements; the system requirements are listed in a system requirements document (SRD). A preliminary design review confirms the overall design of the system, including the requirements of its constituent subsystems and the interfaces between them. A critical design review examines the design of the subsystems and confirms that their components are sufficiently well defined for component design and build to commence. Test readiness reviews confirm that components, subsystems and the system, along with the necessary test environments and test procedures are ready for testing to commence. Finally, a qualification/validation review looks at all the evidence amassed during design, build, integration and testing and qualification and validation to confirm that the system meets its requirements and is fit for purpose, providing a capability which will meet the user's needs and is therefore ready for handover.

c) **Earned value management reviews** are applied on projects using EVM, especially where EVM is a contractual requirement. An integrated baseline review (IBR) assesses the content and integrity of the project's performance management baseline and control processes that will be used during project implementation. An IBR is held late in the mobilisation phase or early in the implementation phase, after the PMB has been established and after at least one progress review cycle. It demonstrates the maturity of the plan, the project team's understanding of it and commitment to it, and the stakeholders' understanding of the risks inherent in it. A demonstration review focuses more on the project's EVM system, checking that it is compliant with the PMP and that it is operating correctly. Surveillance reviews are performed periodically during the remainder of project implementation to confirm that the EVM system is continuing to work correctly.

d) **Life cycle management gate reviews** mark the end of project phases or stages and their function is to check that the project is on course to meet its objectives, and ultimately determine whether the project should be allowed to continue. They are described in Section 6.5.

Effective information management and reporting is necessary for all types of review. Information management is the collection, storage, dissemination, archiving and appropriate destruction of project information. More than just a burden on the project imposed by contractual, governance or legal obligations, it is a value-added activity on which the success or otherwise of the review process hinges. Data must be collected and safely stored before it can be analysed; analysis and dissemination ensure that meaningful information is extracted from the mass of data and arranged in a useful format that facilitates management by exception and effective decision making. So, for example, earned value analysis may reveal variances on a majority of work packages, but most of them may be minor and need only monitoring; only variances of significant magnitude require immediate responses and the information management process should ensure that it is these that are highlighted.

As well as effective information management and reporting, effective review requires:

- **Effective management of the review cycle.** With the project manager focussing on non-recurring project activities, the project support experts are usually best placed to ensure that the drumbeat of periodic reviews continues.
- **Effective facilitation of individual reviews.** Reviews are costly in both time and money: good facilitation ensures that they achieve their objectives with maximum cost-effectiveness. Facilitation includes determining the objectives for each review, defining attendance and an agenda to achieve the objectives, ensuring that attendees are suitably prepared and post-review, ensuring that actions are completed.
- **Effective meeting management.** The meeting chair must ensure that the review meeting is conducted in accordance with its agenda, so that all the necessary business is completed in the time available.

- **Appropriate organisational culture.** The review culture should be challenging but supportive. Good work by the project team should be celebrated and advice and assistance should be forthcoming when necessary.

6.2.5 Change management

The key feature of the closed-loop control of projects is that the control loops *must* be closed: variances from plan will generally only become worse if not responded to, so changes must be made to the project to ensure that variances are addressed. Change management is the process that ensures that all changes to a project's baselined scope, quality/time/cost objectives or agreed benefits are identified, evaluated, approved, rejected or deferred (Figure 16). It includes baselining the project management plan as part of mobilisation.

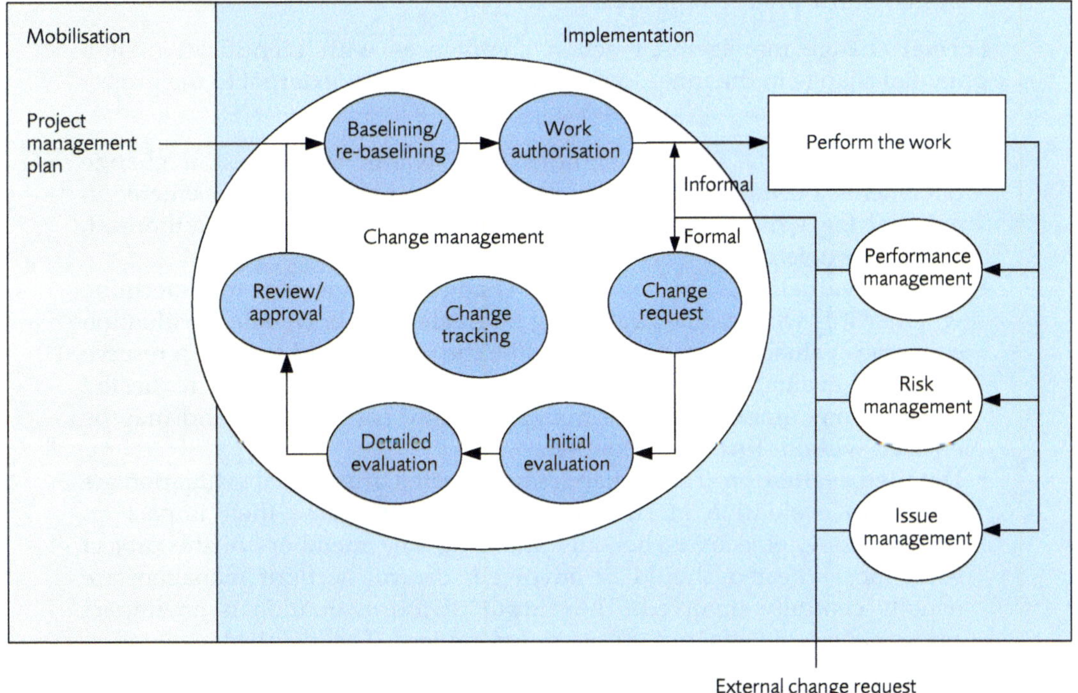

Figure 16: The change management process

Changes may be identified internally or externally to the project. Internal changes are in response to performance variances, risks and issues: they are less likely to affect project objectives and may be resolved within the project's schedule and budget. External changes from the client or organisation are much more likely to affect objectives and, if they do, will require evaluation of their effects on scope, quality/time/cost and benefits.

A lot of routine and minor changes can be managed informally and don't go through the formal change management process; an example might be providing advice and on-the-job-coaching to an inexperienced member of the project team to take a different and better approach to a project activity. More significant changes requiring formal change management action are non-routine and likely to involve significant time and cost; one measure of effective project planning and control is that such changes should be relatively infrequent. Examples of changes requiring formal change management action include:

- internal: the occurrence of a project risk, requiring the implementation of a contingency plan;
- external: a change to the user requirements, requiring a change to the design of the project's products.

Formal change management action commences with identification of a potential change in the inner loop control processes or external to the project and continues with:

- **Change request.** The stakeholder who wants to request a change documents it using a change request form. The change request is entered in a change log, which is a record of all project changes – proposed, authorised, rejected or deferred.
- **Initial evaluation.** The requested change is reviewed to determine whether it is worthwhile evaluating in greater detail. Detailed evaluation consumes valuable resources and while the plan should include a reserve for such evaluations, it should be used judiciously. Some requested changes may quickly be determined to be not cost-effective and may be rejected without further evaluation.
- **Detailed evaluation.** Those changes not rejected after initial evaluation are subject to evaluation in sufficient detail to determine their impact on project scope, objectives, benefits and risk. The members of the project team most affected should be involved; control account managers are usually centrally involved. The output of the evaluation is an impact assessment which is put forward for review. The detailed evaluation should be conducted quickly and the impact assessment should consider the point at which the change will be embodied, because the project will progress while the change is being evaluated, changing the circumstances in which the change has to be introduced.
- **Review/approval.** Review and approval of changes may be left to the project sponsor and project board as one of their standing tasks. On major projects, a change management board may be needed, meeting periodically or

when changes are requested. Change review considers the impact assessment, determines the cost-effectiveness of the requested change and approves or rejects it.

- **Re-baselining.** The impact assessment should sufficiently define the required change so that approved changes can be introduced into the project's baseline plan without significant additional planning work. The required changes to the plan are implemented and the baseline is revised to reflect the changed requirements, scope, schedule and budget. Changes to user requirements require configuration management action.
- **Work authorisation.** Used during mobilisation for initial work packages and subsequently in response to changes, this informs the affected control account managers of the changes to their control accounts and authorises them to commence their new/revised scopes of work.

Effective change management requires that changes are tracked and a change log is used for this, recording the status of changes through identification, request, evaluation, review and implementation. Change logs also record changes to scope, cost and budget to provide a running record of the current baseline with regard to these parameters.

6.3 OUTER LOOP CONTROL PROCESSES

The outer loop control processes together provide a feedback control system for all of the organisation's projects, ensuring that each project is performing correctly, is achieving its objectives and thereby contributing to the required benefits, is benefiting from experience on previous projects and is contributing to the organisation's knowledge base for application to successor projects.

6.3.1 Quality assurance

Quality management of projects consists of quality planning, quality control, quality assurance and continuous improvement. Quality assurance provides confidence to the organisation that quality planning and quality control are correct, so that the project is capable of achieving its quality objectives. Quality assurance is distinguished by formality and independence, the former reflected in the nature of the assurance activities and the latter in the role of quality specialists from outside the project team.

Quality planning is that part of project planning which ensures that the project, during implementation, will be capable of delivering satisfactory outputs, which will be verified by appropriate quality control. Quality planning defines the quality control arrangements in the project management plan (PMP). For larger projects, the quality control arrangements may be broken out into a subsidiary quality management plan (QMP). The arrangements should be consistent with the organisation's quality management system (QMS), applied to the unique needs of the project.

Project planning, including quality planning, is conducted during the concept and (in particular) the definition phases. Quality assurance during these phases must therefore provide confidence that the quality control arrangements being planned for the project are satisfactory. On larger projects, it is usual for quality function personnel to be part of the project team during planning, so that their subject matter expertise can be applied; thus the management plan will define, for example:

- The product realisation processes to be used.
- The product realisation reviews to be conducted.
- The inspections, tests and measurements that will provide the evidence that quality requirements have been achieved.

Quality assurance confirms that the necessary activities are included in the plan. This is achieved by formal review and approval of the project management plan/project quality management plan by a senior representative of the organisation's quality function.

Quality assurance during the other project phases, particularly during implementation, critically examines the project to confirm that quality control is being conducted in accordance with its PMP/QMP. If a senior representative of the quality function is part of the project board, then progress reviews provide a regular opportunity for quality assurance oversight. In addition, periodic (annual, quarterly) conformance audits are conducted to confirm that the quality control arrangements are being adhered to. These are formal reviews, led by quality function personnel independent of the project team. Any deficiencies identified are communicated to the project board and must be addressed by the project manager.

Conformance audits may be supplemented by other, specialist audits to assure other aspects of the project, for example:

- Configuration audits check that all the project products/deliverables conform with one another and with their specifications, to confirm that there is consistency throughout the product documentation.
- Financial appraisal assesses the financial aspects of the project.

6.3.2 Life cycle management

Inner loop review ensures that the status of a project is known to the project manager, the project team, the sponsor/project board and other stakeholders. It is a tactical process, enabling the organisation to confirm that it is doing the project right and to correct it if it isn't. In contrast, life cycle management is more strategic; at key points in the project life cycle, usually at the ends of phases, it enables the organisation to confirm that it is doing the right project, based initially on the project's business case and subsequently on progress towards its objectives. It confirms that those objectives are of continued relevance to the organisation. For the project manager, the most adverse outcome of life cycle management is the termination of the project; however, this may be the correct outcome for the organisation if the evidence suggests that the project will fail to achieve its objectives, or if the objectives are no longer appropriate in a changing organisational environment.

Life cycle management requires an infrastructure:

- The organisation must have an agreed project life cycle model, and while limited tailoring is allowed, projects must be planned and executed in the defined phases.
- There must be an agreed set of gate reviews and the expectations for projects at each review must be defined. The definition includes expectations for planning maturity, performance, retirement of risk, progress towards objectives and a continuing sound business case. The definition also includes the structure of the review and the deliverables required to provide evidence of maturity, performance, etc. Generic pass/fail criteria should be defined.
- Personnel must be trained and experienced in life cycle management. The organisation needs a group of competent reviewers and project managers need to know how to prepare for and conduct themselves during gate reviews.

Such an infrastructure takes significant time, effort and expenditure to develop and once established, must be maintained, with progressive enhancements and continuation training. The investment should be repaid in terms of improved project, portfolio/programme and business outcomes and for an organisation bidding for external contracts, life cycle management is likely to be a prerequisite and potentially a discriminator.

To perform life cycle management:

- **reviewers must be chosen.** Depending on the size, complexity and criticality of the project, the review may require one person or a small team. The lead reviewer is chosen by the sponsor and the project board, in consultation with the project manager. The lead reviewer is typically a highly experienced and successful current or former project manager, not directly involved in the project to be reviewed, with experience of the life cycle management process. The lead reviewer helps define and engage the rest of the review team. The members of the review team are typically highly qualified and experienced and therefore in great demand within the organisation; negotiation may be necessary in order to secure their loan from other projects or functional activities. The review team may include personnel from third parties, potentially including client representation and personnel from key subcontractors;

- **continuity is very beneficial.** Reviewers must understand the project in order to review effectively and this requires familiarity with the project. Familiarity is achieved with least effort if the project's concept phase reviewers continue to review the project through the rest of its life cycle (though there may be a case to revise or supplement the review team to introduce subject matter expertise relevant to particular phases of the life cycle);
- **preparation is essential,** by both the review team and the project manager. If not already familiar with the project, the review team must familiarise themselves, define specific pass/fail criteria, identify any areas of concern and lay down a review timetable. All of these must be communicated to the project manager, who must lead the project team in preparing for the review, preparing deliverables which address the concerns and pass/fail criteria. The deliverables are likely to rely heavily on outputs from the inner loop control processes;
- **reviews must be professionally conducted.** The review team must conduct individual interviews and group meetings in accordance with the review timetable, ensuring that it receives the evidence it needs from the project team. Members of the project team must support the interviews and meetings and promptly complete any actions arising.

Gate reviews may take just hours or even weeks to prepare for and may last from hours to days, depending on the project and the phase. They require time and budget, which must be allowed for in the plan. Depending on the life cycle model adopted by the organisation, gate reviews may include:

- an initiation review, which reviews the project initiation document and determines whether a project should be started;
- a concept review, at the end of the concept phase, which tests the feasibility of the project and the soundness of its business case;
- a definition review at the end of the definition phase, which tests that the project is satisfactorily planned. The existence of a sound and detailed plan is confirmation of the project's feasibility and the cost estimate contained in the plan is a central element of the refined business case;
- a mobilisation review which confirms that the project has been successfully mobilised (launched), with the necessary resources in place and the initial performance measurement baseline established;
- a handover review, which confirms the maturity of the project's products and their readiness for handover to their users; it is closely related to the product realisation qualification/validation review;
- a completion review, which confirms that all the project's products have been realised and that project objectives have been achieved;
- a closeout review, which marks the ultimate completion of the project. Preparation for this review ensures that lessons learned from the project are captured.

There may be additional gate reviews during the implementation phase, linked to product realisation reviews, for example to confirm the successful completion of the product design stage.

Review results and recommendations are presented to the sponsor and project board for decision. The potential review outcomes are:

- **Pass:** the project is allowed to continue to the next phase.
- **Conditional pass:** the project is allowed to continue, contingent on certain changes to the project management plan. Supplemental gate reviews may be held to confirm that the required changes have been successfully implemented.
- **Hold:** the project is not allowed to continue until changes defined by the review team have been implemented. Implementation of those changes is obviously then the priority of the project manager and the project team and a supplemental gate review must be convened as soon as possible.
- **Fail:** the project is terminated. This extreme outcome is obviously not taken lightly, involving the writing off of all project expenditure to date (though partial completion of some project objectives may deliver some returns to the organisation). Termination of a project being performed on behalf of a client has even greater ramifications, requiring negotiation with the client, the likely payment of damages and probable reputational damage. It may nevertheless be the appropriate review outcome for the organisation, if the risks of continuing outweigh any potential benefits.

Where an organisation is bidding for contracts, life cycle management gate reviews are supplemented by contract acquisition reviews (separate reviews or integrated). At the end of the identification phase, a review is held to determine whether the business case for the opportunity justifies the expenditure of internal funds on a pursuit. The end of the pursuit phase is marked by a review to determine whether it is appropriate to bid. The bid phase includes a bid/no bid review, during which the organisation assures itself that it has a viable and potentially winning proposal. Assuming a successful bid, the bid phase ends with review and acceptance of the client's contract. Finally, the project completion review considers completion of the contract.

6.3.3 Continuous improvement

Continuous improvement ensures that successive projects achieve their objectives more efficiently and effectively than their predecessors, while avoiding previous mistakes. It requires the organisation to look within at its project operations and to look outside at its peer group.

The inward-looking element of continuous improvement is the application of lessons learned (Figure 17). This requires the following:

- **Maintenance of a projects knowledge base.** The organisation should maintain a repository of lessons learned and this is typically a project office responsibility. The knowledge base contains many types of information including: examples of good practice (e.g. work breakdown structures, responsibility assignment matrices, schedules); standard costs (labour hours and material costs for regularly-repeated activities); risks (causes and effective responses); problems/issues (causes and effective responses). The knowledge base should ideally be online to facilitate access and should be well-structured for ease of use. The knowledge base also resides in the heads of the organisation's project management community and this should be nurtured by retention of experienced personnel, mentoring of junior personnel, and via selection of project sponsors and life cycle management reviewers.

- **Documentation of lessons learned.** This occurs principally during project closeout, but should be ongoing, with significant arisings documented as they occur. Lessons learned (good and bad), hints and tips and other useful information should be captured and stored. Methods range from a quick e-mail to the project office, through to a comprehensive closeout review of a major project involving all the stakeholders.
- **Optimisation of plans.** Project management plans should be optimised during project concept and definition phases by combining the experience of planning specialists with that of a project manager familiar with the type of project and subject matter experts for the scope of work. The projects knowledge base should be frequently consulted and indeed is likely to expedite planning by providing good practice material that can be re-used in the new PMP. If done well, the PMP should define a project from which many of the potential pitfalls have been designed out.
- **Application of solutions.** The solutions to minor variances and routine problems arising during project mobilisation and implementation are likely to be intuitive to the project manager and the project team. The solutions to most non-routine major variances and problems can usually be derived from scratch, but may well already exist in the knowledge base for identical or similar situations. Application of solutions already in the knowledge base can therefore expedite resolution of variances and problems.

The outward-looking element of continuous improvement entails the organisation seeking to improve the ways in which it manages projects, by benchmarking itself against its peers and against established models of project management maturity, such as the APM publication *Models to Improve the Management of Projects*.[8] Benchmarking identifies and helps prioritise areas for improvement.

[8] Association for Project Management (2007) *Models to Improve the Management of Projects*, APM Knowledge, ISBN: 978-1-903494-80-6

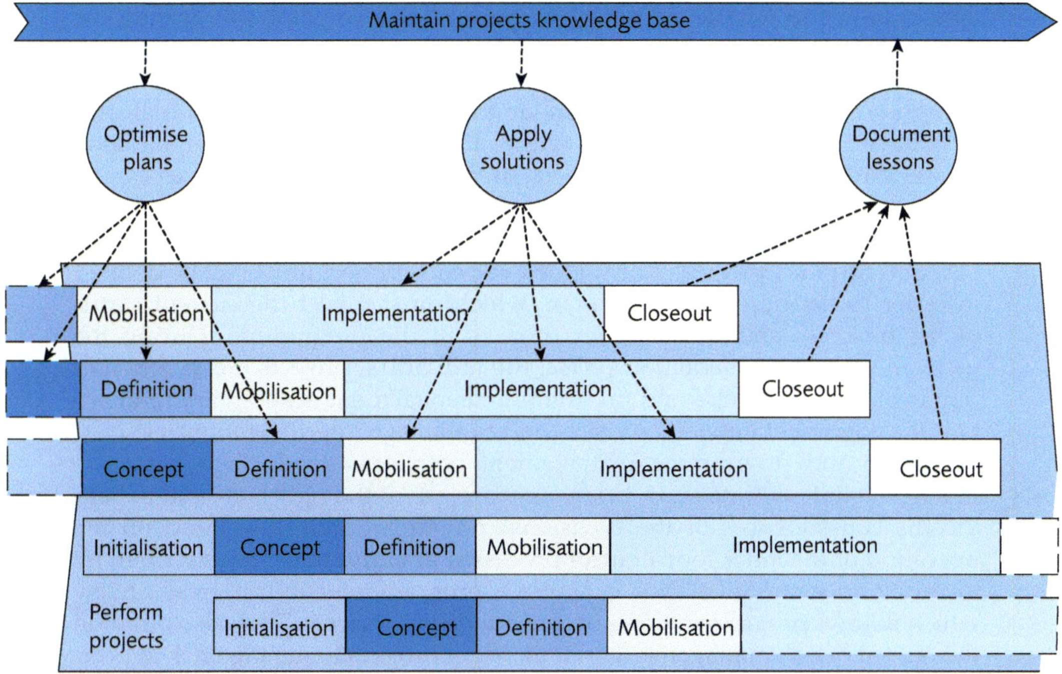

Figure 17: Continuous improvement - applying lessons learned

As with life cycle management, continuous improvement requires an infrastructure to be established and maintained, requiring expenditure of time, and effort and significant cost. The payoff should be improved project outcomes.

6.3.4 Portfolio/programme management

Portfolio and programme management both link projects with the organisation's business strategy, ensuring that the projects being undertaken are consistent with the business strategy and help deliver the strategy. They also link projects with each other, to ensure that each project is not unduly hindered by constrained access to shared resources. In addition, programme management coordinates related projects so that interdependencies are achieved and delivery of the individual projects' objectives contribute to the strategic change needed by the organisation.

Portfolio and programme management involve selection of the projects best able to deliver the business strategy. For portfolios, this involves selection of projects and programmes using criteria such as return on investment, nature of strategic change required and in the case of an organisation pursuing external contracts, which market sectors to engage in and which individual opportunities to pursue. Within programmes, it involves decomposing the required strategic change into manageable chunks that can be delivered via individual projects.

Programmes have a life cycle similar to that of projects; individual projects have their whole life cycles within the programme's implementation phase. Within a programme, projects' initiation and concept phases can be abbreviated, because the concept and definition phases of the programme will already have determined in outline the need for them, their scope, strategy, outline plans and feasibility. However, each project must still be defined in order to develop a detailed plan, which must reflect the current status of the business and of the other projects in the programme. During the programme's implementation phase, the individual projects are at different points in their life cycles and programme management is necessary to maintain the alignment between projects and to manage interdependencies.

Portfolio and programme management both operate through life cycle management to initiate appropriate new projects at the right time and to handle the consequences of the occasional project failure. They build on the operation of the inner loop control processes in individual projects, often by inserting an extra 'level', for example a programme-level progress review which follows progress reviews of the individual projects. They also build on the output of risk management on individual projects to manage risk at portfolio/programme level, either by inclusion of projects' most severe risks in portfolio/programme risk registers or by operation of an organisation-wide risk database.

Organisationally, portfolio and programme management are achieved with additions to the typical project organisation shown in Figure 9. For programmes, there is an extra organisational level: individual project managers now report to a programme manager who reports in turn to a sponsor who chairs a programme-level project board. The programme manager, project managers and project support personnel may be formed into a programme management organisation (PMO) to implement one or more programmes. Project boards are replaced by portfolio or programme boards.

Programme management is addressed in the APM publication *Introduction to Programme Management*[9] and a new publication, *Introduction to Portfolio Management* is in preparation.

6.3.5 Governance of project management

Governance of project management is the ultimate outer loop control process, requiring and enabling all the other control processes to operate and ensuring

[9] Association for Project Management (2007) *Introduction to Programme Management*, APM Knowledge, ISBN: 978-1-903494-63-9

that they do so effectively. It does this by defining the principles and components of project management governance for the organisation, which must be addressed by the organisation's senior leadership ('the board').

Eleven governance of project management principles and four main components of project management governance are defined in the APM publication *Directing Change: A Guide to the Governance of Project Management.*[10] Several of the eleven governance principles relate directly to project control:

- Principle 3: "Disciplined governance arrangements, supported by appropriate methods and controls, are applied throughout the project life cycle." This establishes the need for project control(s), acknowledges the existence of the project life cycle and requires control to operate throughout.
- Principle 9: "There are clearly defined criteria for reporting project status and for the escalation of risks and issues to the levels required by the organisation". This principle establishes that projects will be reported and by requiring that reporting criteria are defined, establishes the need for a common approach across the organisation, appropriate use of metrics, etc. It also establishes the need for risk and issue management and for escalation from project level to higher levels of the organisation.
- Principle 10: "The organisation fosters a culture of improvement and of frank internal disclosure of project information". This establishes the need for continuous improvement and acknowledges that an appropriate culture in necessary for effective control.

The four components of governance are:

1. Portfolio direction, which seeks to ensure that all projects are identified within the organisation's portfolio and that the portfolio is optimised with regard to the organisation's aims and constraints.
2. Project sponsorship, which ensures, via sponsorship of projects that there is an effective link between the organisation's senior leadership and its project managers.
3. Project management effectiveness and efficiency, which seeks to ensure that the teams responsible for projects are capable of achieving project objectives which are defined at project approval points.
4. Disclosure and reporting, which ensures that project reports provide timely, relevant and reliable information that supports the organisation's decision making, without micro-management.

The APM publication *Directing change: A Guide to the Governance of Project Management* poses questions to the organisation about its implementation of the four components of governance. Establishing and maintaining project

[10] Association for Project Management (2004) *Directing Change: A Guide to Governance of Project Management*, APM Knowledge, ISBN: 978-1-903494-26-4

management arrangements, including project control processes which provide satisfactory answers to these questions, ensures that the organisation's management of projects works well.

6.4 APPROPRIATENESS, FREQUENCY, METRICS AND REPORTS

6.4.1 Appropriateness

The application of control processes to an individual project must be appropriate to the project and to the phase of the project. Control in each life cycle phase has already been addressed in Section 4.

In applying the control processes to an individual project, the default assumption should be that all of the processes will apply. The processes are the organisation's way of controlling projects and satisfying its governance requirements and there should therefore be few exceptions. It may be that very small projects are excluded from the full suite of control processes and the organisation's governance arrangements may set a value threshold below which exceptions are allowed. However, there should be flexibility in terms of process techniques used; the aim of the control processes is to assist the project manager and the project team and through them the sponsor and the rest of the organisation, to conceptualise the status of the project, to identify problem areas as quickly as possible and correct them. The specific techniques used should therefore be relevant, appropriate and cost-effective; they should be neither so simple that they overlook significant problems, nor so complex as to confuse matters and consume excessive resources. So, for example, a small project may not require earned value management and a simple spreadsheet may suffice as a risk register.

A project manager's experience in project control, often aided by that of project support experts and applied within the organisation's governance arrangements, determines the techniques appropriate to the project. The techniques should be selected during detailed planning in the definition phase and the gate review at the end of the definition phase should examine whether the selected techniques are appropriate. Considerations include the following:

- **Project size/cost and complexity.** Large, high-cost projects are not necessarily complex, though they are more challenging because of their scale. The factors increasing complexity apply to projects of all sizes and include application of new technology, a diverse scope of supply and a complex supply chain. Large size/cost and complex projects typically require additional control both directly, because of their scale and complexity and indirectly, because of their greater significance to the organisation.
- **Project uncertainty and risk.** Uncertain or risky projects are likely to require additional control, to reduce uncertainty and risk to levels acceptable

to the organisation and to other key stakeholders. Novelty increases uncertainty, i.e. when an organisation undertakes a project of a type for which it has no prior experience.
- **Project criticality.** A project may be of high criticality to the organisation, for example, a 'must succeed' contract or a key internal change project. Organisations are likely to require additional control effort on such projects.
- **Time and resources available for control.** Control must be accomplished within constraints of available time and resources – but the project manager and the sponsor must ensure that these are sufficient.

Application of processes and choice of techniques should be undertaken with care to avoid damaging the integrity of the control processes. The process owners (typically the project office) should be consulted. Decision trees may be used to formalise the organisation's policies about appropriateness, e.g. if budget is more than £1M use earned value management and Monte Carlo simulation. Process owners should remain alert for application developments potentially relevant to future projects, which indicate where the standard processes may be improved.

6.4.2 Frequency

The frequency at which the control processes operate varies from hourly at one end of the spectrum to annual or less at the other. For example:

- the project team should respond to performance problems as soon as they are identified, i.e. in close to real time;
- the progress review cycle is determined for the project, but is often the on in general use within the organisation. Monthly, linked to financial periods is typical, however, some organisations operate performance measurement on a fortnightly or even a weekly basis;
- other reviews are non-recurring, taking place once per project at the appropriate point in the project life cycle or product realisation process;
- quality assurance reviews and governance reviews may take place each quarter, bi-annually or annually.

Figure 18 gives an impression of the relationship between frequency and formality of control activities during project implementation.

Important and/or time-critical projects may need to be measured and reviewed (at least in part, e.g. critical path and key milestones) more frequently than other projects.

A challenge, particularly on larger projects, is to balance the time necessary to formally measure performance and to prepare for reviews with the need to review up-to-date information. The review preparation time includes some of the most value-added parts of project control: identifying variances, understanding what's going on and defining appropriate corrective actions. On the other hand, if too long is spent on this, the information being reviewed will become out of date and the danger is that the next review cycle will be commencing before the current review cycle has been completed. The project manager, in agreement with the sponsor and the project board, need to recognise this conflict and strike a balance appropriate to the needs of the specific project. However, the needs of each individual project may be subsumed by the need to integrate project reviews into programme/portfolio reviews and into business reporting cycles.

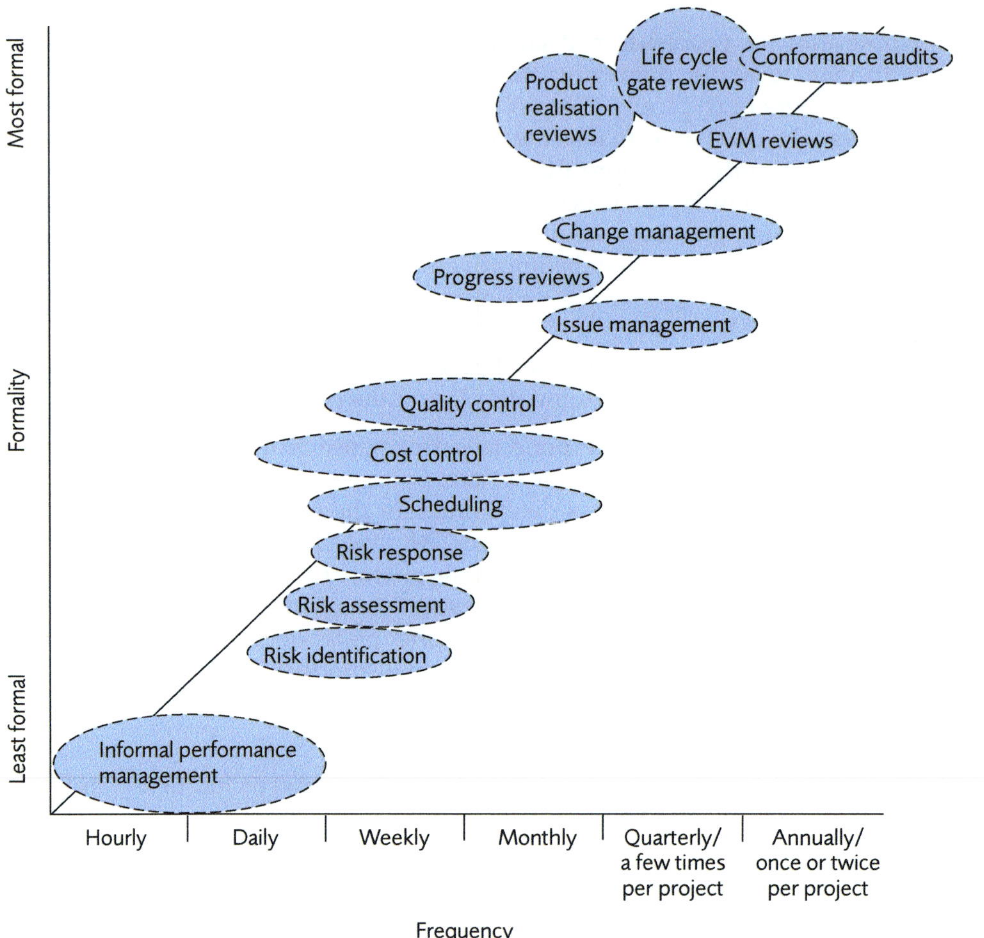

Figure 18: Frequency and formality of control activities

6.4.3 Metrics and reports

The fourth component of the governance of project management, disclosure and reporting, establishes the need for timely, relevant and reliable reporting to support decision making without micro-management. Anything other than the smallest project, in applying quantitative control processes, generates copious amounts of data which could overwhelm the project team, the project manager and the sponsor. Somewhere in the mass of data is likely to be important information about significant variances, risks and issues; this key information needs to be identified, extracted and used. It is important to extract useful information from the mass of data to synthesise an holistic view of project status. This is achieved by appropriate choice of metrics and by the design of suitable reports.

A metric is a measure of a performance parameter. A range of metrics should be selected to reflect all aspects of the project and each should ideally be presented showing its current actual value, a history of previous values and a forecast of future values, all referenced to a target or budget. Traffic light colours can be used, i.e. using red to highlight major concerns, amber for some concerns and green for no concerns. Key performance indicators (KPIs) and critical success factors (CSFs) in particular should have metrics. Examples of metrics include the following:

- **Quality:** lines of software code completed; percentage of requirements now with evidence of conformance.
- **Time:** proportion of key milestones on schedule; estimated project completion date.
- **Cost:** actual cost; estimate to complete and at completion; amount of management reserve remaining.
- **Risk:** quantity of risks by risk factor; overall cost impact of risks; Monte Carlo simulation showing earliest likely, most likely and latest likely completion dates.
- **Issues:** quantity unresolved; average time to resolve issues.

Earned value management provides a set of metrics in the form of schedule and cost variances and indices. If EVM is implemented well, these metrics encompass quality performance as well as time and cost, since it will be impossible to complete work and claim earned value without achieving the quality requirements applicable to that work.

Metrics are assembled into reports for use in reviews, generally by project support experts on behalf of the project manager. Reports for progress reviews should contain sufficient metrics to show the status of the project, in combination with value-added commentary to highlight the significance of the metrics. Time should be set aside prior to reviews for the project manager to consider the metrics and to determine their significance, to identify any necessary actions and to prepare a concise summary of project status. This preparation should enable progress reviews to proceed quickly and effectively. The intent should be to inform the sponsor and other stakeholders, avoiding surprises and enabling management by exception. Progress reports should be signed by the project manager and sponsor as a formal record, providing evidence for quality assurance and governance purposes.

7
Conclusions - characteristics of good project control

Even the simplest human endeavours (such as bike trips) require control. Projects are unique, transient endeavours undertaken to achieve desired outcome and need control because they are inherently unstable; without control, they tend to depart from their plans making it unlikely that their objectives will be achieved. Small variances grow to large ones unless the causes are quickly fixed. Projects are also inherently risky because they are unique, constrained, complex, based on assumptions and performed by people.

A narrow definition of project control is:

> "The application of processes to measure project performance against the project plan, to enable variances to be identified and corrected, so that project objectives are achieved."

This is essentially about doing projects right, and primarily involves inner loop control processes residing within the project. A wider and more complete definition of project control is:

> "The application of project, programme and portfolio management processes within a framework of project management governance to enable an organisation to do the right projects and to do them right."

Project control operates across a spectrum from the tactical to the strategic, involving much of the overall discipline of project management and also most of the individual project management disciplines represented by APM's Specific Interest Groups. Among the dependencies on the individual disciplines, truly effective control is only possible when effective project planning has been undertaken; a good project management plan is vital for effective control because it defines 'the management' and 'the plan'. Project control measures variances from 'the plan' ('what', 'how much' and 'when') and applies corrections via 'the management' ('how', 'who' and 'where').

Project managers must control their unique, transient and unstable projects in order to achieve their objectives, and most of what a project manager does during the life of a project has a 'control' element to it. Project managers apply 'soft' skills (leadership, influencing, negotiation, etc.) but must also use the 'hard', quantitative processes, using feedback to achieve closed loop control, that are the main focus of this publication.

At one end of the spectrum, the control processes are mostly reactive, high frequency, relatively informal and largely internal to the project; the other end of the spectrum is more proactive, lower frequency, more formal and external to the project. The processes blend from pure project control through control/management of portfolios and programmes into the organisation's business management processes and corporate governance – from tactical to strategic, from 'control' to 'management' and from 'inner loop' to 'outer loop'.

The inner loop control processes are:

1. Performance management, which is the measurement of project activities in the quality, time and cost dimensions, the analysis of the performance revealed by the measurements, and the identification of suitable responses to variances from plan revealed by the analysis. Performance management focuses on what's happening now and in the recent past and may need to trade among the quality, time and cost dimensions.
2. Risk management, which is forward looking and seeks to avoid threats and maximise opportunities. It identifies and measures risks, determines appropriate responses to them and implements the responses.
3. Issue management, which identifies and addresses those problems that cannot be resolved within the project, escalating them to obtain external assistance.
4. Review, which ensures that the status of the project is known to the project manager, the project team, the sponsor/project board and other stakeholders.
5. Change management, which ensures that all changes to a project's scope, quality/time/cost objectives or agreed benefits are identified, evaluated, approved, rejected or deferred. This avoids the potential for uncontrolled change called scope creep.

Within performance management, earned value management is the single most powerful technique.

While the inner loop control processes reside within a single project, the outer loop control processes wrap around all the organisation's projects and provide the organisational framework and context within which individual projects are undertaken. The outer loop processes are:

1. Quality assurance, which provides confidence to the organisation that quality planning and quality control are correct, so that the project is capable of achieving its quality objectives. Quality assurance is distinguished by formality and independence, the former reflected in the nature of the assurance activities and the latter in the role of quality specialists from outside the project team.

2. Life cycle management, which, at key points in the project life cycle, enables the organisation to confirm that it is doing the right project, based initially on the project's business case and subsequently on progress towards its objectives.
3. Continuous improvement ensures that successive projects achieve their objectives more efficiently and effectively than their predecessors, while avoiding previous mistakes. This requires the organisation to maintain a projects knowledge base, and also to look externally to compare itself with peers and project management maturity models.
4. Portfolio and programme management both link projects with the organisation's business strategy, ensuring that the projects being undertaken are consistent with the business strategy and help deliver the strategy. They also link projects with each other, to ensure that each project is not unduly hindered by constrained access to shared resources. In addition, programme management coordinates related projects so that interdependencies are achieved and delivery of the individual projects' objectives contribute to the strategic change needed by the organisation.
5. Governance of project management, which is the ultimate outer loop control process, requiring and enabling all the other control processes to operate and ensuring that they do so effectively.

Portfolio management, programme management and the governance of project management are all much more than control processes; their identification here as outer loop control processes is intended only to explain their roles in project control.

The application of the control processes to an individual project must be appropriate to the project and to the phase of the project. They should be conducted at an appropriate frequency and to produce an holistic view by use of carefully-chosen metrics and value-added reports.

The fundamental reason for control is to maximise the chances of project success, through achievement of the project's objectives – and to demonstrate that this has been achieved. Good control helps avoid many of the common reasons for project failure and is relevant in different ways to different types of organisations involved in projects.

An understanding of the project life cycle is fundamental to project control. Project control starts even before the project starts: an initiation phase enables the organisation to confirm the need for a project. The outer loop control processes wrap around all projects and operate for as long as an organisation is undertaking projects. The inner loop control processes reside within individual projects but apply selectively in different phases of the project life cycle. The relative importance of the inner and outer loop control processes, the effort expended on them and, particularly, their leverage on the successful outcome of a project vary throughout the life cycle.

The project manager is, of course, the key figure in project control and the bulk of the control work is performed by the project team. Project support experts carry out a lot of the inner loop processes. However, effective control engages all stakeholders in the project. The role of the sponsor is particularly important in establishing an environment within which effective control is possible.

Hopefully, it is evident that control is non-trivial; is an intellectual process which should harness the full knowledge, experience and potential of the organisation, with all the lessons it has learned, measurements it has made and new ideas it can muster. Good control:

- should look to the future, aiming to avoid problems rather than waiting and having to solve them by fire-fighting;
- is more than just monitoring: a poorly-performing project that's intensively monitored will not turn around without effective corrective action. The control loops must be closed;
- is dependent for its success on an appropriate organisational culture – challenging but supportive; seeking solutions, not trying to apportion blame;
- should provide confidence to stakeholders that the project can achieve useful objectives and should lead to the project being terminated if it cannot;
- depends on an organisational infrastructure obtained through experience and investment, which is a vital asset to organisations performing projects.

Ultimately, even the best control cannot guarantee project success. Foreseen risks do occur and events which could not have been foreseen during the project concept and definition phases may occur and hinder the achievement of project objectives. The project manager must then draw on all the attributes of effective project management to achieve the best outcome for the organisation. But while no guarantee of success, good project control is one of the best ways of avoiding project failure.

It is reckoned that riding a bike once learned is never forgotten. But good control needs to be embedded in the organisation, through appropriate culture, well-documented processes and effective training – and requires constant practice. While the application of control should be appropriate to the size and complexity of the project, some form of control is always required and the more complex and critical the project, the more important project control becomes. With expert control, even complex projects can be completed successfully.

ANNEX A
Abbreviations

ACWP	Actual cost of work performed
APM	Association for Project Management
BCWP	Budgeted cost of work performed
BCWS	Budgeted cost of work scheduled
CAM	Control account manager
CDR	Critical design review
CFE	Client (or contractor)-furnished equipment
CPI	Cost performance index
CSF	Critical success factor
CV	Cost variance
DCF	Discounted cash flow
EAC	Estimate at completion
ETC	Estimate to completion
EVM	Earned value management
GoPM	Governance of project management
IBR	Integrated baseline review
IRR	Internal rate of return
ISO	International Standards Organisation
ITT	Invitation to tender
KPI	Key performance indicator
NPV	Net present value
OBS	Organisation breakdown structure
PBS	Product breakdown structure
PDR	Preliminary design review
PERT	Programme evaluation and review technique
PID	Project initiation document
PMB	Performance measurement baseline
PMO	Programme or portfolio management office

PMP	Project management plan
PSO	Project, programme or portfolio support office
QA	Quality assurance
QC	Quality control
QMP	Quality management plan
QMS	Quality management system
QVR	Qualification/validation review
RAM	Responsibility assignment matrix
RMP	Risk management plan
ROM	Rough order of magnitude
RR	Requirements review
SIG	Specific Interest Group
SoW	Statement of work
SPI	Schedule performance index
SRD	System requirements definition/document
SV	Schedule variance
TRR	Test readiness review
URD	User requirements definition/document
WBS	Work breakdown structure

ANNEX B
Glossary of project planning and control terms

Acceptance The formal process of accepting a **product/deliverable**, e.g. by the **sponsor** from the **project manager** or the **client** from the **contractor**.

Acceptance criteria The requirements and essential conditions that must be achieved before a **product/deliverable** is accepted.

Accrual Work done for which payment is due but has not been made.

Activity The smallest self-contained unit of work in a project's **scope of work**; activities require time (have a finite duration) and consume resources.

Actual cost Cost incurred, charged against the project budget, for which payment has been made or accrued.

Actual cost of work performed (ACWP) A term used in **earned value management**: the cumulative actual cost of project activities up to a particular point in time. For some purposes, cost may be measured in labour hours rather than money.

ADePT A technique for planning and controlling design and engineering projects which accounts for the iterative nature of design/engineering, while planning the information flow through such projects and identifying key design decisions.

Baseline The definition at a moment in time of a project including all parameters of **scope**, quality, cost and time, providing a reference against which actual performance can be measured and **variances** identified.

Benchmarking The review of what other organisations are doing in the same area. For those organisations who appear to be particularly successful in what they do and how they do it and are taken as examples to be emulated, i.e. used as benchmarks.

Benefit An improvement arising from the capability provided by project **products/deliverables** perceived as positive by a stakeholder. Benefits may be tangible (quantifiable and measurable) or intangible.

Benefits management The identification of the **benefits** (of a project or programme) at organisational level and the tracking of the realisation of those benefits.

Bid A **tender, quotation** or other formal offer made to enter into a **contract**.

Bidding The process of preparing and submitting a **bid**.

Bottom-up estimating An **estimating** technique based on making estimates for every work package (or activity) in the work breakdown structure and summarising them to provide an overall estimate of the effort and cost required.

Brainstorming The unstructured generation of ideas by a group of people in a short space of time.

Brief A concise outline (strategic specification) of stakeholders'/clients' needs and objectives for a project.

Budget A sum of money or hours assigned to cover the costs of a project or one of its constituent control accounts or work packages, within which the activity owner is required to work. A project budget includes a **performance management baseline** budget and a **management reserve**.

Budgeted cost of work performed (BCWP) A term used in **earned value management**: the planned cost of work completed to date – the '**earned value**' of the work completed.

Budgeted cost of work scheduled (BCWS) A term used in **earned value management**: the planned cost of work that should have been completed to date, in accordance with the project baseline – the '**planned value**' of the work that should have been completed.

Budget estimate An approximate **estimate** prepared in the early phases of a project to establish financial viability or to secure resources.

Budgeting and cost management The **estimating** of costs and the setting of an agreed **budget**; the management of actual and forecast costs against the **budget**.

Business as usual An **organisation's** normal day-to-day operations (taken to mean non-project operations).

Business case A statement, owned by a **sponsor**, of the justification for undertaking a project, evaluating the benefit, cost and risk of alternatives and the rationale for the preferred solution. Its purpose is to obtain management approval and commitment for investment in the project.

Calendar A project calendar defines time intervals in which activities or resources cannot be scheduled. A project usually has a default calendar for the normal work week (e.g. Monday to Friday), but it may use other calendars as well. Each calendar is customised with its own holidays, additional work days or different working hours. Resources and activities can be attached to any of the calendars.

Capability maturity model An organisational model that describes a number of evolutionary levels in which an organisation manages its processes, typically ranging from ad hoc (lowest maturity level) to continual improvement of processes (highest maturity level).

Cash flow forecast A prediction of the difference between cash received and payments made during a specific period or for the duration of a project.

Champion Someone who acts as an advocate for a proposal or a project, spearheads an idea or action and 'sells it' through the organisation. Someone in an organisation who promotes or defends a project, such as its **sponsor**. Also, an end **user** representative seconded into a project team to represent the needs of the user community.

Change freeze A point in the **project life cycle** after which no further changes will be considered.

Change log (or register) A record of all project changes – proposed, authorised, rejected or deferred.

Change management The discipline and formal process through which changes to the project plan are approved and introduced. Also, the process by which organisational change is introduced.

Change request A request to obtain formal approval for changes to a project.

Charter A document that sets out the working relationships and agreed behaviours within a **project team**.

Client The party to a **contract** which commissions work and pays for it on completion.

Client (or contractor)-furnished equipment (CFE) Equipment provided by a client to a contractor, or by a contractor to a subcontractor, as free issue for use in a project.

Closeout phase The fifth **phase** of the **project life cycle** (after the **concept**, **definition**, **mobilisation** and **implementation** phases, and after the pre-project **initiation phase** and project start) during which project matters are finalised, final **project reviews** are carried out, project information is archived and the **project team** is **demobilised** and re-deployed. The closeout phase may occur before implementation is completed, or even earlier, if the project is terminated. At the end of the closeout phase, the project is finished.

Commissioning The advancement of an installation from the stage of static completion to full working order and the achievement of the specified operational requirements.

Commitment A binding financial obligation, typically in the form of a purchase order or contract; the amount of money removed from the budget by this obligation.

Communication The giving, receiving, processing and interpretation of information. Information can be conveyed verbally, non-verbally, actively, passively, formally, informally, consciously and unconsciously.

Comparative estimating An **estimating** technique based on the comparison with, and factoring from, the cost of a previous similar project or operation.

Competitive tendering A formal **procurement** process whereby **vendors** or **contractors** are given an equal chance to **tender** for the supply of goods or services against a fixed set of rules.

Concept phase The first **phase** in the **project life cycle** (after the pre-project **initiation phase** and project start), during which the need, opportunity or problem is confirmed, the feasibility of the project is considered and a preferred solution identified.

Configuration Functional and physical characteristics of a **product/deliverable** as defined in technical documents and achieved in the product.

Configuration audit A check to ensure that all **products/deliverables** of a project conform with one another and with the current specification. It ensures that the relevant **quality assurance** procedures have been implemented and that there is consistency throughout the project's documentation.

Configuration management The discipline and process concerned with the creation, maintenance and controlled change of **configuration** throughout the project or product life cycle.

Conflict management The discipline and process of identifying and addressing differences which if unmanaged would affect project objectives. Effective conflict management prevents differences becoming destructive elements in a project.

Conformance audit An audit of the operation of a project to ensure that the defined processes are being adhered to.

Constraints Restrictions considered as fixed or which must happen that will affect a project.

Contingency A planned allocation of time or budget for unforeseeable **risks** in a project; something held in reserve for the unknown.

Contingency budget An amount of money set aside to implement a **contingency plan**.

Contingency plan An alternative course of action to be adopted if project risks occur or expected outcomes are not achieved.

Continuous improvement A business philosophy popularised in Japan where it is known as Kaizen. It creates steady improvement by keeping an organisation focussed on its goals and priorities; a planned and systematic approach to improvement on an on-going basis.

Contract A mutually binding agreement in which the **contractor** is obligated to provide goods or services and the client is obligated to pay for them.

Contractor A person or organisation who holds a **contract** for the provision of goods or services.

Contract price The price payable by the client to the **contractor** for the proper delivery of the goods or services specified in the **contract**.

Corrective action Action taken to correct a **variance**, to bring project performance back into line with the plan.

Control account A defined subset of a project's **scope of work**, usually a set of **work packages**, assigned to a **control account manager**.

Control account manager An individual responsible for the completion of a **control account** to quality, time and cost objectives and responsible for managing the necessary resources.

Cost-benefit analysis An analysis of the relationship between the costs of undertaking an activity or project, initial and recurrent, and the benefits likely to arise from the changed situation, initially and recurrently.

Cost estimating The process of predicting the costs of a project.

Cost performance index (CPI) A term used in **earned value management**: the ratio of the planned cost of work completed to date (the **earned value**) to the cumulative actual cost of completing the work (i.e. BCWP ÷ ACWP). CPI is an efficiency rating for the work completed versus the resources expended.

Cost performance report A regular report providing information on project cost and schedule status.

Cost variance (CV) A term used in **earned value management.** It is the difference between the planned cost of work completed to date (the **earned value**) and the cumulative actual cost of completing the work (i.e. BCWP-ACWP).

Critical chain A networking technique based on Goldratt's theory of constraints that identifies paths through a project based on resource dependencies as well as technological precedence requirements.

Critical path The sequence of activities through a project from start to finish, the sum of whose durations determines the project's duration. There may be more than one such path. The path through a series of activities, taking into account **interdependencies**, in which the late completion of any of the activities will have an impact on the project finish date or will delay a key **milestone**.

Critical path analysis The procedure for calculating the critical path and floats in a network/schedule.

Critical path method A technique used to predict project duration by analysing which sequence of activities has the least amount of scheduling flexibility.

Critical success factor (CSF) See **success factor**.

Culture The attitudes and values which inform and guide the actions of those involved in a project.

Cut-off (or status) date The end date of a reporting period providing a reference point for financial and other performance information.

Definition phase The second **phase** of the **project life cycle** (after the concept **phase**, and after the pre-project **initiation phase** and project start), during which the preferred solution is further evaluated and optimised. Often an iterative process, definition can affect the project's requirements, scope and quality/time/cost objectives.

Delegation The practice of getting others to perform work effectively that one chooses not to do oneself. The process by which authority and responsibility are distributed by a manager to subordinates.

Deliverable (or product) A tangible intermediate or final output of a project.

Delphi technique A process where a consensus view is reached by consultation with experts. Often used as an estimating technique.

Demobilisation The controlled dispersal of personnel when they are no longer needed on a project.

Demonstration review A review of a project's **earned value management** system to confirm that it is compliant with the requirements defined in the **project management plan** and is operating correctly.

Dependency Something on which the successful delivery of a project depends. An external dependency is one outside the scope of the project, for example in another project.

Design authority The person or organisation with overall design responsibility for specified products.

Design stage The stage in the project's implementation phase where the design of the project's products is determined.

Deviation A departure from the plan or the requirements.

Discounted cash flow (DCF) The concept of relating future cash inflows and outflows over the life of a project or operation to a common base value, thereby allowing more validity in the comparison of different projects with different durations and rates of cash flow.

Disposal stage A stage in the implementation phase of an extended project during which the project's products/deliverables are removed from use, de-commissioned and disposed of, with due concern for realisation of any residual value, re-use, recycling and other environmental considerations.

Earned value A term used in **earned value management**: the planned cost of work completed to date, i.e. the **budgeted cost of work performed (BCWP)**. A measure of project progress, it may be expressed in terms of money or labour hours.

Earned value analysis An analysis of project progress where the value of the work achieved is compared with the actual cost incurred. The analysis is conducted at various levels of the **work breakdown structure** to identify any elements of the **scope of work** with significant **variances**.

Earned value management A discipline and process based on a structured approach to planning, cost collection and performance measurement. It facilitates the integration of project **scope**, time and cost objectives and establishes a baseline plan against which performance can be measured.

Earned value management system The tools and techniques for measuring, analysis and reporting **planned value**, **earned value** and actual cost whereby **earned value management** is implemented.

End user A person or organisation that will use the products/deliverables of a project.

Escalation The process by which aspects of a project (for example **issues)** are drawn to the attention of those senior to the project manager, such as the **sponsor** and the **project board**.

Estimate A prediction or forecast, e.g. of the time and cost required to perform a defined **scope of work**. Generally made prior to project **implementation**, it can be refined during implementation.

Estimate at completion (EAC) A prediction or forecast of final cost on completion of all work, expressed in terms of money or labour hours, generally made after **implementation** has commenced.

Estimate to complete (ETC) A prediction or forecast of the cost that will be incurred in completing remaining work, expressed in terms of money or labour hours, generally made after **implementation** has commenced.

Estimating The use of a range of techniques and tools to produce **estimates**.

Extended life cycle A **project life cycle** which includes additional **phases** or **stages**, such as **operation** and **disposal** of project **products/deliverables**.

Feasibility study An analysis to determine if a course of action is possible within defined terms of reference; work carried out on a proposed project or alternatives to provide a basis for deciding whether to proceed.

Financial appraisal An assessment of the financial aspects of a project or **programme**.

Fitness for purpose The degree to which **products/deliverables** satisfy **user/stakeholder** needs.

Force field analysis A technique used to identify the various pressures promoting or resisting change.

Forecast An **estimate** or prediction of future conditions or events based on information and knowledge available when the forecast is prepared.

Function The natural action or intended purpose of a person or thing in a particular role. A part of an **organisation** containing specialist resources performing a particular role, e.g. marketing, engineering, finance, information technology.

Functional analysis The identification and analysis of the functional attributes of different solutions.

Functional manager (or head of function) The person responsible for the business and technical management of an organisational function.

Funding The money available for expenditure on a project, from an organisation's internal funds or from an external **contract**, providing the project **budget**.

Gate review A formal review of a project during its **life cycle** where its plan, progress, expected cost and expected value are reviewed and a decision is made whether to continue to the next **phase** or **stage** of the project.

Goal A concise definition specifying what will be accomplished, incorporating an event signifying completion.

Governance of Project Management (GoPM) GoPM concerns those areas of corporate governance that are specifically related to project activities. Effective governance of project management ensures that an organisation's

portfolio is aligned with the organisation's objectives, and is delivered efficiently and sustainably.

Handover The point or period in the **life cycle** where project **products/deliverables** are handed over to the **sponsor** and **users**.

Impact analysis An assessment of the effect on project objectives of a proposed change or of a **risk** occurring.

Implementation phase The fourth phase of the **project life cycle** (after the **concept**, **definition** and **mobilisation** phases, and after the pre-project **initiation phase** and project start), during which the **project management plan** is executed to realise the **products/deliverables** and to hand them over. The implementation phase includes **product realisation** and **handover** stages and, on extended projects, also includes **operation** and/or **disposal** stages.

Initiation phase A generally short pre-project **phase** during which a **project initiation document** is prepared, which enables the **organisation** to confirm the need for a project. If the need is confirmed, a **project manager** is assigned with suitable terms of reference and a budget for the resources required for the **concept phase**; a project is started and the concept phase (the first **phase** of the **project life cycle** proper) commences.

Information management The collection, storage, dissemination, archiving and appropriate destruction of project information.

Integrated baseline review (IBR) A review following the establishment of the initial **baseline**, to ensure that it is comprehensive and correct and understood by the **organisation**.

Interdependency A mutual dependency between one or more projects, which must be satisfied if the dependent projects are to succeed.

Investment An outlay of money, time or other resources, usually for income, profit or other benefit; such as the capital outlay for a project.

Investment appraisal The determination of the value of a project, involving cash flow forecasting, discounted cash flow analysis and the calculation of payback period and internal rate of return (IRR).

Invitation to tender (ITT) An invitation to a supplier to tender or bid for the provision of goods or services.

Issue A problem threatening project **objectives** which cannot be resolved by the project manager.

Issue log A log of all the issues raised during a project, showing details of each issue, its evaluation, what decisions were made and its status.

Issue management The discipline and process by which issues are identified and addressed to remove the threats that they pose to project **objectives**.

Key performance indicator (KPI) See **performance indicator**.

Last Planner A technique for identifying short-term 'look ahead' **schedules** based on a master schedule, and analysing constraints on activities which may prevent them being completed in accordance with the **master schedule**. The technique includes robust measures of progress of the rate at which activities in the schedule are completed.

Leadership The ability to establish vision and direction, to influence and align others towards a common purpose, and to empower and inspire people to achieve success. It enables a project to proceed in an environment of change and uncertainty.

Learning and development The continual improvement of competencies in the **organisation**. The identification and application of learning within projects develops the organisation's capability to undertake current and future projects.

Lessons learned The identification of activities that went well, and those that could have been better, to recommend improvements to be applied in the future and to future projects.

Life cycle See **project life cycle**.

Liquidated damages The liability in a **contract** to pay a specified sum for a breach of contract, such as the late delivery of goods or services.

Litigation Any lawsuit or other reason to resort to court to determine a legal question or matter.

Make or buy decision The decision to make a **product** internally or to buy it from a supplier. For example, whether to develop a software application in house or to purchase an existing software application off-the-shelf.

Management by exception A term used to describe management of problem areas only.

Management reserve A sum of money held as a contingency to cover the cost impact of problems, such as the occurrence of a threat to project objectives. A project's management reserve may be sub-divided, e.g. into a specific risk provision (for identified and specific adverse risks) and a non-specific risk provision (for potential emergent adverse risks).

Marketing Publicising and promoting an organisation in pursuit of new business; anticipating the demands of users and satisfying their needs by providing goods and services or the right quality at the right time and cost (e.g. by performing a project).

Master schedule A high-level summary project **schedule** identifying major **activities** and **milestones**.

Metric A measure of a performance parameter such as a **performance indicator** or a **success factor**. A metric should ideally be presented showing its current actual value, a history of previous values and a forecast of future values, all referenced to a target or budget.

Milestone A key event selected for its importance in the project.

Mobilisation phase The third **phase** of the **project life cycle** (after the **concept** and **definition** phases, and after the pre-project **initiation phase** and project start). The mobilisation phase is a relatively short, transitional phase between definition and **implementation**, during which the **project team** is brought together, equipment and facilities are secured, the plan is baselined and the initial implementation phase **work packages** are authorised. At the end of the mobilisation phase the project can be regarded as 'launched'.

Model A way of looking at reality, usually for the purpose of abstracting and simplifying it, to make it understandable in a particular context. Models may be either physical or virtual.

Monitoring The recording, analysing and reporting of project performance as compared to the plan in order to identify and report deviations (NB. here subsumed into 'control').

Monte Carlo simulation A technique used to estimate the likely range of outcomes from a complex process or project, by simulating the process under randomly-selected conditions a large number of times.

Need, problem or opportunity The underlying reason for undertaking a project; without a defined and agreed need, problem or opportunity, a project should not be started.

Negotiation A search for agreement, seeking acceptance, consensus and alignment of views. Negotiation can be informal or formal, such as in the agreements of terms and conditions for a contract.

Network analysis A method used to calculate a project's **critical path** and activity times and float.

Non-recurring costs Expenditures against specific activities expected to occur only once in a given **project**, **programme**, **portfolio** or **organisation**.

Objectives Desired results towards which effort is directed.

Operation stage A stage in the **implementation phase** of an **extended project**, during which the **products/deliverables** are operated by the **end users** for their intended purpose and are maintained.

Opportunity An uncertain event which might favourably impact on a project's objectives; an 'upside', beneficial **risk**.

Order of magnitude/rough order of magnitude (ROM) estimate An **estimate** carried out to give a very approximate indication of expected cost.

Organisation A single corporate entity undertaking some combination of **projects**, **programmes**, **portfolio(s)** and **business as usual**.

Organisational breakdown structure (OBS) A hierarchical representation of a organisation, decomposing the organisation into successively small groups, used for planning and control purposes.

Organisation design The design of the most appropriate organisation for a particular purpose, e.g. of a project team for a specific project.

Outcome The result of a project or the result of a deliberation concerning part of a project.

Outputs Deliverables that are the result of a process.

Outsourcing The contracting out or buying in of facilities or work (rather than using in-house resources).

Parametric estimating An estimating technique that uses a statistical relationship between historical data and other variables (for example floor area in construction, lines of code in software development) to calculate an estimate.

Pareto technique A technique to identify the minority of variables with the greatest impact on project objectives (known as 'the 80:20 rule').

Performance indicator A measure of success that can be used throughout a project to ensure that it is progressing towards a successful conclusion. The most important of these are identified as key performance indicators (KPIs).

Performance management The discipline and process of managing the performance of activities, individuals and organisational groups; also, a term used in **earned value management**, which is itself a performance management technique applied to projects.

Performance measurement baseline (PMB) An approved, integrated scope/schedule/budget plan for a project, with which performance is compared, so that variances can be identified and addressed.

Phase (of a project) One of a series of steps that together constitute the **project life cycle**; a logical sub-division of the life cycle, at the end of which a required degree of completion, maturity and risk retirement and/or a defined set of intermediate or final **products/deliverables** has been achieved. During a phase, a set of related and inter-linked activities are performed to achieve a designated objective.

Phase review A formal **review** of a project at the end of a **life cycle phase** where its plan, progress, expected cost and expected value are reviewed and a decision is made whether to continue to the next phase.

Planned value A term used in **earned value management**: the cost of work intended to be completed to date, i.e. the **budgeted cost of work scheduled (BCWS)**. A measure of a project's planned progress, it may be expressed in terms of money or labour hours.

Planning The process of identifying the means, resources and actions necessary to accomplish an objective.

Portfolio A grouping of an organisation's **projects, programmes** and related **business as usual** activities.

Portfolio management The selection and management of all an **organisation's projects, programmes** and related **business as usual** activities to achieve the organisation's strategy, taking into account resource constraints.

Prime (or lead) contractor An **organisation** holding the **contract** for much or all of an endeavour. The prime contractor is responsible for managing the whole endeavour, including managing the work of any **subcontractors**, integrating their **products/deliverables** and managing **risks** to meet the **client's** requirements.

Problem A concern that can be resolved by the **project manager** and the **project team** within the **scope** of the project.

Procurement The process by which resources (goods and services) are acquired by one **organisation** from others. It involves development of the overall procurement strategy, strategies for individual procurements, preparation of contracts, selection and acquisition of suppliers and management of contracts.

Product (or deliverable) A tangible intermediate or final output of a project.

Product realisation stage The stage of a project's **implementation phase** during which the **products/deliverables** are created.

Product breakdown structure (PBS) A hierarchical decomposition of the **products/deliverables** comprising the **scope of supply** of a project.

Programme A group of related projects, which may include related **business as usual** activities, together intended to achieve a beneficial change of a strategic nature for an **organisation**.

Programme management The coordinated management of a **programme**.

Programme (or portolfio) management office (PMO) An organisational grouping responsible for the business and technical management of a **programme** or a **portfolio**.

Programme manager The individual responsible and accountable for the successful delivery of a **programme**.

Project A unique, transient endeavour undertaken to achieve a desired outcome.

Project appraisal An evaluation of the viability of a project, which may be carried out at any time during the project's **life cycle**.

Project assurance Independent monitoring and reporting of the project's performance and **products/deliverables**.

Project board A steering group for one or more projects whose remit is to set the strategic direction for the project(s) and to provide guidance to the **sponsor** and the **project manager**. The project board represents the interests of the **organisation**, and assists the sponsor in assuring that the project is satisfactorily performed.

Project context The environment within which a project is undertaken. Projects do not exist in a vacuum and an appreciation of the context within which a project is being performed assists the **project manager** to deliver it.

Project control The application of processes to measure project performance against the project plan, to enable variances to be identified and corrected, so that project objectives are achieved (narrow definition). The application of project, programme and portfolio management processes within a framework of project management governance to enable an organisation to do the right projects and to do them right (wider definition).

Project director The manager of a very large project that demands senior level responsibility, or the person at board level in an **organisation** with overall responsibility for **project management**.

Programme evaluation and review technique (PERT) A technique for determining how much time a project needs to complete.

Project financing and funding The means by which the capital to undertake a project is initially secured and then made available at the appropriate time. Projects may be financed externally, funded internally or be a combination of both.

Project initiation document (PID) A document defining the terms of reference for a project and which must be approved by the **project board** in order for the project to start.

Project life cycle The sequence of **phases** and **stages** between the start and finish of a project, which may also be considered to include an **initiation phase** preceding project start. All projects follow a **life cycle**. Adherence to a life cycle enables a project to be considered as a sequence of distinct phases and stages that provide the structure and approach for progressively delivering the required outputs. Life cycles may differ between industries and business sectors but an organisation typically uses a single life cycle **model** as part of its **project control** arrangements.

Project management The process by which projects are defined, planned, monitored, controlled and delivered so that agreed benefits are realised.

Project management maturity A **model** that describes a number of evolutionary levels in which an **organisation's project management** processes can be assessed, from ad hoc use of processes to **continual improvement** of processes.

Project management plan (PMP) A plan that brings together all the plans for a project. The purpose of a PMP is to document the outcome of the planning process and to provide the reference document for managing the project. The project management plan is owned by the **project manager**.

Project manager The individual responsible and accountable for the successful delivery of a project.

Project objectives Those things that are to be achieved by the project, which usually include technical, quality, time and cost dimensions and may include other items in accordance with **stakeholder** needs.

Project planning The process of identifying the means, resources and actions necessary to accomplish a project.

Project office An organisational grouping of functional specialists (e.g. **project support experts**) which serves an **organisation's project management** needs. A project office can provide a range of services from support for the **project manager** to responsibility for linking an organisation's strategy to its project execution. Project office types include: project support office, **programme management office**, **portfolio management office**.

Project review calendar A calendar of project **review** dates, meetings and issues of **reports**, set against calendar dates, financial periods or project week numbers.

Project support experts Individuals with expertise in particular aspects of project support such as scheduling, budgeting, cost management, earned value management and reporting.

Project support office (PSO) See **project office**.

Project team A set of individuals, groups and/or organisations reporting to a **project manager**, established for the purpose of delivering a project. Individuals may be seconded from their organisational functions to work in a multi-disciplinary team, bringing with them their **subject matter expertise**. A project team may be co-located (a 'four walls team').

Qualification Demonstration that the **products/deliverables** meet the necessary technical standards.

Quality Fitness for purpose or degree of conformance with **requirements**.

Quality assurance (QA) The process of evaluating project performance on a regular basis to provide confidence that the project will satisfy the relevant quality **requirements**.

Quality audit A formal examination to determine whether practices conform to specified standards, or a critical examination of whether a **product/deliverable** meets quality criteria.

Quality control (QC) The process of monitoring specific project results to determine if they comply with relevant standards, and identifying ways to eliminate causes of unsatisfactory performance.

Quality criteria The characteristics of a **product/deliverable** that to determine whether it meets **requirements**.

Quality management (for a project) The discipline that is applied the ensure that both the **products/deliverables** of a project and the processes by which the products/deliverables are realised meet their **quality requirements**.

Quality management plan (QMP) (for a project) That part of the **project management plan** that defines the **quality management** arrangements for the project.

Quality management system (QMS) The complete set of quality standards, procedures and responsibilities for an **organisation**.

Quality planning The process of determining which quality standards are applicable and how to apply them.

Quality review A review of a **product/deliverable** against an established set of quality criteria.

Recurring costs Expenditures against specific activities expected to occur repeatedly in a given **project**, **programme**, **portfolio** or **organisation**, for example in producing multiple instances of an individual **product/deliverable**.

Reporting The formatting and presentation of information to communicate project status to **stakeholders**.

Reports A written record or summary; a detailed account or statement, or a verbal account; a compilation of information in an appropriate format.

Request for proposal/quotation (RFP/RFQ) A document used to request proposals from prospective vendors of goods and services.

Requirement Something demanded or imposed as an obligation, or a stated need, e.g. of a **product/deliverable** (form, fit, function, cost etc.).

Requirements management The process of capturing, analysing and testing the stated needs of a **client/user/stakeholder**.

Resource An item required to undertake an activity, such a suitably qualified and experienced person, a piece of equipment or a facility. Use of resources incurs costs and hence requires budget.

Resource allocation The process by which resources are mapped to the activities which require them.

Resource calendar A project calendar specific to an individual resource or group of resources defines time intervals in which the resources available for project activities.

Resource management The discipline and process that identifies and assigns **resources** to activities so that projects can be undertaken with acceptable levels of resources in an acceptable duration, within the overall resources available to the **organisation** as a whole and with regard to constraints on the use of those resources.

Resource planning The process of identifying, assigning, and levelling the **resources** needed by a project to enable the project to be undertaken with available resources in an acceptable duration.

Responsibility assignment matrix (RAM) A diagram or chart showing assigned responsibilities for elements of work, created by combining a **work breakdown structure** with an **organisation breakdown structure**.

Review A critical examination of a project undertaken to assess actual and projected performance against objectives, typically, but not necessarily, conducted in a review meeting.

Risk action owner An individual who has responsibility for action(s) which are part of the response to risk(s).

Risk (event) An uncertain event which might impact on a project's objectives, negatively in the case of **threats** and favourably in the case of **opportunities**.

Risk factor A numeric or alphanumeric designation of the severity of a **risk (event)** on an defined scale. The risk factor is one consideration in determining the priority that should be accorded to responding to the risk, and determines how the risk should be reported.

Risk management (for a project) The discipline that is applied the ensure that individual **risks (risk events)** and overall **project risk** are understood and proactively managed, optimising project success by minimising **threats** and maximising **opportunities**.

Risk management plan (RMP) (for a project) That part of the **project management plan** that defines the **risk management** arrangements for the project.

Risk manager An individual in charge of matters connected with **risk** for a **project, programme, portfolio** or **organisation**.

Risk owner An individual who has responsibility for dealing with a particular **risk (event)**.

Risk (project) The exposure of project **stakeholders** to the consequences of variation in outcome arising from the summation of all individual project **risks**.

Risk register (or log) A body of information listing all the **risks (risk events)** identified for a **project, programme, portfolio** or **organisation**, explaining the nature of each risk and recording information on its assessment, potential impact and management. A risk register is normally maintained throughout the **life cycle** of a project/programme/portfolio, and on an on-going basis for an organisation.

Risk retirement The progressive elimination of **project risk** until at the finish of the project, with all objectives completed, none remains.

Rolling wave planning An approach to planning in which only the current **phase, stage** or time period of a project is planned in detail, future phases being planned in outline only. Each phase produces a detailed plan for the next phase.

Schedule The timetable for a project, showing how project activities and **milestones** are planned over a period of time. Schedules are usually presented as a Gantt or other bar chart, but milestone charts or tabular listings of dates can be used as well or instead.

Schedule performance index (SPI) A term used in **earned value management**; the ratio of the planned cost of work completed to date (the **earned value**) to the planned cost of work that should have been completed to date (the **planned value**) of the work that should have been completed (i.e. BCWP ÷ BCWS). SPI is an efficiency rating for the work accomplishment, comparing work achieved to what should have been achieved at any point in time.

Scheduling The process used to control the time dimension of a project, determine the sequence of activities in the project and its overall duration. This includes determining the logical **interdependencies** between activities and estimating activity durations, taking into account requirements and available resources.

Schedule variance (SV) A term used in earned value management. The difference between the planned cost of work completed to date (the **earned value**) and the planned cost of work that should have been completed to date (the **planned value**) (i.e. BCWP - BCWS).

Scope The totality of a project, including its **scope of supply** and **scope of work**.

Scope creep Gradual and uncontrolled growth or change of project **scope**.

Scope management The discipline and process that is applied to ensure that the **scope** of a project, including both **scope of supply** and **scope of work**, is identified, defined and controlled. Identification and definition of scope must describe what a project includes and also what it will not include, i.e. what is in scope and out of scope.

Scope of supply The totality of the tangible **products/deliverables** (goods and services) to be provided by a project. The scope of supply can be defined using a **product breakdown structure**.

Scope of work The totality of the work of a project. The scope of work can be defined in a **statement of work**, often by using a **work breakdown structure**.

Sensitivity analysis An investigation of the effect on the outcome of changing parameters or data.

Simulation A process whereby some dynamic aspect of a **system** or project is replicated (modelled) without using the real system, often using computerised techniques.

Sponsor An individual or body for whom a project is undertaken and who is the primary risk taker. The sponsor owns the **business case** and is ultimately responsible for the project and for delivering its benefits.

Sponsorship An active senior management role, responsible for identifying business needs, problems or opportunities. A sponsor ensures that a project remains viable and that benefits are realised, resolving any issues that are outside the control of the **project manager**.

Slip (or trend) chart A pictorial representation of how the forecast and actual completion dates of project **milestones** have changed over time, typically from one periodic progress **review** to the next.

Stage One of a series of steps that together constitute a **phase** of the **project life cycle**; a logical sub-division of the life cycle, at the end of which a required degree of completion, maturity and risk retirement and/or a defined set of intermediate or final products/deliverables has been achieved. During a stage, a set of related and inter-linked activities are performed to achieve a designated objective.

Stage payment A payment made part-way through a project on completion of a pre-determined **milestone**, such as on completion of a **life cycle stage** or **phase,** or on completion of a particular **product/deliverable**.

Stakeholder An individual or **organisation** with an interest or role in a project, influence over it or impact on it. Stakeholders with the largest interest, role or influence are called key stakeholders.

Stakeholder analysis The identification of **stakeholders**, their interest levels and their ability to influence a project.

Stakeholder management The discipline and process that is applied to ensure that **stakeholders** are systematically identified and analysed and that actions are planned and undertaken to communicate with, negotiate with and influence them.

Statement of work (SoW) A document defining the totality of the work of a project, often by using or including a **work breakdown structure**.

Status report A description of where a project currently stands, usually in the form of a document, issued by the **project manager** to **stakeholders** on a regular basis, outlining the status of part or all of the scope of work. It may be a formal report on the input, issues and actions resulting from a progress or status meeting.

Subcontract A contractual document that legally transfers the responsibility and effort of providing goods, services, data or other **products/deliverables** from one **organisation** (the **contractor**) to another (the **subcontractor**).

Subcontractor An **organisation** that provides goods, services, data or other **products/deliverables** to another (the **contractor**) under a **subcontract**.

Subject matter expert An individual with specialist expertise, knowledge and experience in a discipline or functional area.

Success criteria The qualitative and quantitative measures by which success is judged.

Success factors Things present in a project's environment that are conducive to and necessary for the success of the project. The most important of these are identified as critical success factors (CSFs).

Supplier A **subcontractor**, consultant or other **organisation** providing resources to an organisation.

Supply chain management The discipline and process that is applied to strategically and tactically manage all other **organisations** providing goods, services, data or other **products/deliverables** to an organisation.

System An integrated set of **products/deliverables** which function together to provide a required capability.

Team An organisational grouping of two or more people working interdependently towards a common goal.

Technology management The discipline and process managing the relationship between emerging and available technologies, an **organisation** and its projects. It includes the management of enabling technologies necessary for organisational processes and projects and of technologies included in products/deliverables.

Tender A document proposing to provide defined goods or services in a defined way and at a stated price (or on a particular financial basis); an offer of price and conditions under which a supplier is prepared to undertake work for a **client**.

Termination Early closeout of a project, before expected completion, due to poor performance or changing circumstances.

Testing The process of determining how aspects of a **product/deliverable** perform when subjected to defined conditions.

Threat An uncertain event which might unfavourably impact on a project's objectives; a 'downside', adverse **risk event**.

Three point estimate An estimate in which an optimistic value (quickest, cheapest), a most likely value and a pessimistic value (slowest, most expensive) are all defined.

Top down cost estimating An **estimate** of project cost based on historical costs and other project variables, sub-divided down to individual **work packages** or activities.

Traffic light report A type of report that highlights current status by use of traffic light colours, i.e. using red to highlight major concerns, amber for some concerns and green for no concerns.

Uncertainty A state of incomplete knowledge, usually associated with **risks**.

User An individual, usually one of a group of users, for whom **products/deliverables** are intended and who will operate them after handover.

User requirement Something demanded or imposed as an obligation, or a stated need, e.g. of a **product/deliverable** (form, fit, function, cost etc.), by a **user**, usually relating to a new capability required by the user.

Validation Confirmation that **products/deliverables** meet **users'** needs, usually by demonstration or trial involving the users.

Value engineering Optimisation of the conceptual, technical and operational aspects of **products/deliverables**.

Value management The discipline and process of defining what value means to an **organisation**. It allows needs, problems or opportunities to be defined and then analysed to determine the optimal approach and solution to satisfying them.

Variance A discrepancy from the **baseline** plan, e.g. of quality, time or cost performance.

Verification Confirmation that **products/deliverables** meet their requirements, which is obtained by inspection, testing or demonstration.

Work breakdown structure (WBS) A hierarchical decomposition of the **scope of work** of a project, for the purposes of project planning and control. The WBS sub-divides the overall scope of work until a level of detail necessary for planning and control is achieved. The lowest units of the work breakdown structure are generally **work packages**.

Work package Generally the lowest unit of a project's **work breakdown structure**, containing a logical grouping of related activities, suitable for the purposes of planning (e.g. **bottom-up cost estimating**) and control (e.g. performance measurement, cost collection).

ANNEX C
Further Information

The *APM Body of Knowledge, 5th edition* and the other references contain extensive reading lists and bibliographies identifying many sources of further information about project control.

Further information on APM and its Specific Interest Groups can be found on the APM website at www.apm.org.uk

ANNEX D
Information about the APM Planning SIG

Membership and mission

The APM Planning Specific Interest Group (SIG) consists of representatives of the aerospace and defence, construction, nuclear and rail sectors, as well as cross-sector project managers. The members of the SIG believe that good project planning is critical to project success and should therefore be at the heart of the project management process. Accordingly the APM Planning SIG should be considered as a link between existing APM SIGs.

The APM Planning SIG's mission is to advance and raise the profile and professionalism of project planning, by:

- documenting and disseminating best practice;
- instigating debate in APM and elsewhere on planning practice;
- advancing the state of the art;
- enhancing educational frameworks for planning;
- reinforcing the professionalism and enhancing the standing of planners;
- contributing to future issues of the *APM Body of Knowledge*.

Next steps

The APM Planning SIG is keen to receive feedback on this *Introduction to Project Control* from the project management community and from planning and control practitioners in particular, to inform future editions.

The APM Planning SIG intends to proceed with the development of an APM *UK Guide to Project Planning and Control,* which will provide the basis for foundation qualification(s) in project planning/control. A more-detailed practitioners' guide and associated practitioners' qualification(s) are expected to follow.

Why join the APM Planning SIG?

Membership of the APM Planning SIG is open to all APM members and to representatives of corporate members who have a particular interest in project planning.

As a member of the APM Planning SIG, you will:

- be part of the leading UK group addressing project planning matters;
- be able to share views and concerns and exchange information with other planning professionals;

- participate in the development of best practice, guidance, standards and educational frameworks for project planning;
- help to foster relationships with business and with other professional groups.

How to join

Contact us via planningsig@apm.org.uk for further information.

Association for Project Management

Ibis House, Regent Park
Summerleys Road
Princes Risborough
Buckinghamshire, HP27 9LE

Telephone 0845 458 1944
International +44 (0)1844 271640
Facsimile +44 (0)1844 274509

Email info@apm.org.uk
Web www.apm.org.uk

ISBN-10: 1-903494-34-6
ISBN-13: 978-1-903494-34-9

ND - #0144 - 080726 - C104 - 246/189/5 - PB - 9781903494349 - Matt Lamination